The Pepperpot Club

The Pepperpot Club
Jonathan Phang

hardie grant books

MELBOURNE · LONDON

My dear R—:— Since I came to
I often think of you & what it
would mean to you should
the opportunity. Though I t
I can only imagine you se
do for good & your brot
Since then the far side v
you occasionally. I am se
would a whole lot you
was away from Home —
& all your Home ties
the Lord of a great Mothe
never tires speaking of yo
Kind folks here & how w
thinks you will get on w
people you may meet. I
that opinion also, but you

For Christopher, Kimberley, Dominic, Joseph, Lauren and Sandie.

This book is dedicated to the memory of my devoted parents and my brother Nicki with eternal thanks and more love than I ever knew.

Contents

My parents were immigrants to London
from the British Colony of Guyana.

Introduction

I spent the first four years of my life eating meals surrounded by old newspapers which had been laid down ready to mop up falling morsels of food that hadn't quite reached my mouth. When relations visited, they would follow me about, wielding damp cloths so they could clean up my trail of mess. To this day, I remain as clumsy an eater as I was when I was four years old! Luckily, my unfortunate habits were ignored at home where eating was more important than untidiness. Apart from my mother's occasional gripes about the food stains I sometimes left on her soft furnishings – bought with hard-earned money – that were supposed to last a lifetime, my parents took great pride in my healthy appetite.

My parents were immigrants to London from the British Colony of Guyana. Although in South America, Guyana is an English-speaking country about the size of the UK and is considered to be a part of the Caribbean. Guyanese people are made up of the six races of the Caribbean: East Indian, Chinese, Mixed European (Creole, mostly British and Portuguese), African, North American and indigenous Amerindian. My grandparents' passports described them as being 'mixed natives of British Guyana'.

Between them, my parents' blood represented all of these six races and they displayed many common characteristics associated with Caribbean Creole, Chinese and British cultures. Temperaments and meals were cross-cultural, diverse and, in some ways, incongruous. When I went to my school friends' homes, I realised my home life was much more dramatic than theirs. Voices were deeper, laughter was louder, music more rhythmic, food was abundant, aromatic and spicy. I learnt to expect bland, badly cooked food away from home. From an early age, I understood that mealtimes represented far more than mere sustenance. Each meal was symbolic of moments important to my family's history and testament to our loved ones. They were accompanied by stories from a place referred to as 'home'. And so, there I was, a perfect blend of these cultures. 'A rainbow child' of the Commonwealth.

The Chinese adore chubby babies of which I was a great specimen. The Caribbeans love feeding people and, as I grew up, my Caribbean aunts gauged the level of my affections for them by how much of their food I ate; so unsurprisingly, I became obsessed with food at an early age. By the age of six I had formed strong opinions about seasoning, the perfect texture of sponge cakes and the buttery flakiness of pastry. As I got older, I enjoyed long conversations with my mother about why some of my aunts' dishes tasted better or worse than others. It also became apparent that I was a little different to other boys my age. Furthermore, I was the youngest of three children and no one really had the time to play with me, so I spent all of my spare time in the kitchen experimenting with food, with its textures, colours

REVENUE ONLY
Odontodenia Grandiflora
$5
Guyana
SOUTH AMERICA

We often spent Sundays in
Chinatown. Starting off
with Dim Sum and sometimes
we stayed on for a whole
afternoon or an early dinner.

and smells, and I loved it. At school, my favourite class, naturally, was home economics. I learned with gusto to make all the things my mother couldn't (and wouldn't!) cook, like puff pastry, butterfly cakes and eventually, Paris-Brest.

Mum had the ability to make anything taste wonderful and was the mistress of improvisation. However, the one virtue she lacked in the kitchen was patience. She was always in such a rush to shop for the food, get it onto the table on time, finish the washing up, do the ironing and take us kids to various clubs, so making pastry or fiddling about with puff pastry leaves, choux buns or sugar roses was not high on her list of priorities! In later years, Mum took great pride in showing off my pastry skills and used to beg me to make patties, pine tarts and sunflower biscuits (traditional Guyanese teatime treats) for our visitors. My parents were very sociable and our home was usually full of relatives and friends who would be expected to stay for whatever meal was being prepared when they arrived. (Lunch often turned into dinner as dish upon dish appeared, seemingly effortlessly produced by Mum.) Weekends were chaos. Dad was a dentist and ran a Saturday morning surgery in the front room of the adjoining semi-detached house. My mother acted as nurse/receptionist and basic all-round dogsbody for my father's practice.

Somehow, between patients, my mother would tear across the front garden and into our kitchen where she'd pull on an apron and instruct me on what to do with whatever she was cooking for Dad's lunch (and whoever else had turned up). Dad expected his lunch to be served to him within minutes of placing his instruments in the steriliser. So my poor Mum worked, cooked and cleaned – but always looked glamorous – while Dad ate lunch sitting with his feet up in front of the television, watching the horse racing, making bets or putting the world to right with his old mates. Female visitors joined Mum and me in the kitchen where they sat around the table and talked non-stop about life, love and home. I listened to all of this, absorbing their tales and their gossip. Then, when Mum had finished cooking the main meal, I would come into my own and bake a cake or make pastry treats. I found that my creations won me approval and gave me something to hide behind as I brought them into the front room for the men to eat.

In contrast to the hectic Saturdays, our Sunday mornings were luxuriously languorous. We'd all have a lie in and then wait, excitedly, while Mum prepared her special scrambled eggs. Us kids would sit on Mum and Dad's bed and he'd place a forkful of scrambled eggs, laced with crispy smoked bacon, onion and hot pepper sauce, on crunchy buttered toast and feed us, one by one, a mouthful at a time. After that we'd all get dressed into our 'special' clothes as Sundays were also the days for going out.

We often spent Sundays in Chinatown, starting off with dim sum and sometimes we stayed on for a whole afternoon or an early dinner. Whichever restaurant we happened to be in, Dad would hold court like some triad warlord while various men would come over for a catch-up. These Chinese and Caribbean immigrants had also come to London in the 1950s and were people my parents had known previously in Georgetown, the capital of British Guiana;

or they were friends they'd met at the West Indian social club in Earl's Court when Dad was a student dentist at Guy's Hospital. Dad was the only one of this group who'd become a professional man and his blue-collar friends admired his position and treated him with awestruck respect, common to that generation. Dad enjoyed the attention and played the role of an affluent bon viveur to the full, arriving in his fur-collared car coat, smoking a fat cigar. He did, however, genuinely love meeting people and socialising even more. He was a great raconteur and generous host. His charitable nature was part of his character but also came from the awareness that he felt lucky to be comfortably off. He never forgot the hardship that he and his fellow men met on their arrival in the UK. He was fortunate in that he had the backing of his brothers to see him through his education, a beautiful and dutiful wife at his side and three children who were yet to send him to an early grave.

Often, on the way home after one of these lunches, Dad would decide that we needed to see different parts of London. He'd drive miles out of our way, giving us historical facts about the area he had chosen to visit. Invariably it was a ruse to take us to see a restaurant or café that he and Mum had frequented while courting. But romance after arriving in London wasn't as straightforward as it sounds. Dad was three-quarters Chinese and a quarter Indian. Mum was Creole, meaning half local white and half mixed race (my maternal grandmother was a white Barbadian of Scottish and Portuguese descent). My maternal grandfather was a dark-skinned mix of Amerindian, Barbadian, Scottish and Dutch.

Mum was 15 when she met my Dad, who was eight years her senior. It was love at first sight, although they didn't start dating secretly until a year later. My parents' courtship was the stuff of legend in Georgetown and is remembered by a whole generation to this day. Their first encounter was on the seawall when Mum was on her way home from St Roses (the local convent school) and Dad was liming (the art of doing nothing) with his two brothers and some other local 'sweet boys' (otherwise known as playboys). Both their families opposed this Romeo and Juliet-style romance. My mother's side didn't like my dad because he was eight years her senior and Chinese. My father's family, on the other hand, was against it because the Chinese didn't like to 'dilute' their genes and kept themselves to themselves. They thought mixing races led to weak genes, madness and a whole array of illnesses.

My father's family history was rich and lurid. It included stories of girls being kidnapped and of ships sailing to far-off lands with a laden cargo of silk and tea. This history intrigue was hard for us to believe as kids living in our 1970s' west London suburban semi-detached house. In the early 1840s, slaves taken from Africa to work in Guyana's sugar plantations by the British were emancipated. Without slave labour, the sugar plantation owners were forced to offer contracts of indenture to labourers from Madeira, India and China. The first Chinese men arrived in Guyana in 1853, mainly from Canton. No women were allowed until a decade later.

My father's great great grandfather, Li Lee, was one of the original Chinese

Dad enjoyed the attention and played the role of the affluent bon viveur to the full. arriving in his fur collared car coat smoking a fat cigar.

Mum had the ability to make anything taste wonderful and was the mistress of improvisation. However the one virtue she lacked in the kitchen was patience.

migrants. Li had one son, William Lee (my great grandfather), with an Indian lady named Gann, who he met at his plantation. William Lee married a young Chinese girl named Piat, whose mother (Elizabeth Poon) also had a story that we couldn't quite believe for its hardship!

My mum's family also didn't want my parents' relationship to prosper. First of all, they believed that the paler the skin, the greater the prospects for a person in life and so frowned upon mixed marriages. My mother was the fairest skinned of her siblings and the extended family had high hopes for the young beauty.

My maternal grandfather Cyril was an unhappy, volatile man who had the acid taste of disappointment in his mouth and had been brought up viciously by his own parents. His mother, a Scottish Jew called Mary Elma Clarke, was hard and cruel to her children. She loathed that her children were born dark-skinned; she never smiled and used to beat her children with a broomstick. As a father and husband, Cyril was volatile and violent. He attempted to split Mum and Dad up by beating Mum badly, by enforcing early curfews, and even by cutting up her dresses. Eventually, seeing that Mum wasn't going to stop seeing my dad, Cyril arranged for her to sail to England. Cyril thought that the pressure of a long-distance separation would put an end to their love affair. So, when Mum was only 18 years old, my grandfather packed her bags, dragged her to the docks and sent her off to her new life in a Fulham boarding house in the Mother Country.

Cyril had inadvertently chosen the best possible landlady for mum. Doris was a recently widowed, very jolly Scottish woman with an empty terraced house. Her children were grown up and married and she had no one to look after. She and her husband had spent a couple of years in Georgetown where she enjoyed the trappings of an expat life while he worked for Tate & Lyle, so she understood Mum's background.

This larger-than-life maternal figure offered bed, breakfast and dinner. Doris cooked a hearty fry-up every morning with stews or pies for dinner and, of course, fish and chips on Fridays. Puddings were, invariably, stodgy offerings drenched in Bird's custard. Mum, was, of course, too polite to say anything about this food and didn't know what had hit her. Within a matter of weeks her flimsy, homemade cotton dresses were bursting at the seams.

Uncle John had found Mum a clerical job in the head office at Lyons. She spent all her wages buying new clothes for her ever-expanding waistline. She also needed to buy clothes that would keep her warm! When she couldn't afford to feed the greedy gas meter, she would keep warm in the cinema watching the same film over and over again.

Mum missed my dad desperately and dreamed of being his wife and having plenty of plump Chinese babies. She longed for her mother's company and she worried about her siblings. She was also desperate for fresh fruit, curry and pepperpot. In fact, any food that had some flavour!

Meanwhile, back in Georgetown, Cyril was glowing with triumph and used to cycle up and down the seawall trying to get a glimpse of my father's

William Lee, my great grandfather.

To Dear Roy
With All my love
Maureen

Both their families opposed this Romeo and Juliet style romance.

lovesick face. He didn't want some 'Chiney boy' interfering with his one valuable possession.

Cyril had bigger plans for the fairest skinned of his children. He wanted Mum to have a terrible time in 'that cold miserable country' and to return home humbled, subdued, obedient and ready to marry a man of his choice. However, Cyril's gloating didn't last long. Eight months after Mum's departure, Roy Phang was nowhere to be found. Cyril somehow found out that Roy had sailed to London and immediately wrote to Mum's landlady describing Roy as an untrustworthy, licentious womaniser. However, Doris loved her Georgetown girl and when Dad first arrived in London she let him stay for a bit. Her love of my mum made it easy for her to help the young couple.

It was several years before Mum saw her mother Maude again. When she next saw her, she was shocked and saddened. Marriage to Cyril combined with the loneliness of being so far apart from her children had taken its toll. The once statuesque, auburn-haired beauty had turned into a grey-haired overweight woman. Uncle Reggie settled in St Vincent and Aunty Margaret moved to Barbados. Uncle John left for England, aged 16, and joined the British Army. He never returned to Georgetown.

By now, Maude's beloved housekeeper, Alverine, had died leaving her entirely alone all day while Cyril went to work. She consoled herself by reading romantic novellas and cooked enough food for an army, all the while day dreaming of her beloved children opening the gate and running into the house, hungry and wolfing down her lovingly prepared dishes. By this time, she and Cyril had separate bedrooms and she plastered pictures from magazines of Cary Grant, Gregory Peck and George Peppard all over her bedroom walls so she could be surrounded with romantic possibilities before going to sleep. Maude often sat in the empty kitchen and ate the meals she'd prepared, or took a plate to her room and ate some little treat, planning what to cook for the next day.

Cyril, did, however love Maude and told me many times the story of when he first set eyes on her beautiful face and her shiny, waist-length auburn hair. He outlived Maude by 14 years and missed her with all his heart for each and every one of those 5,110 days. However, when she was alive, typical to his class, race and generation, he treated Maude as nothing more than a domestic servant, no matter how much he loved her. I remember Granny Maude as a kind, pretty and gentle giant with a very comfortable lap to sit in and be cuddled. She used to feed me curry laced with margarine and it would burn my throat, but the thrill of these warm encounters filled me utter joy.

So, it was into this heady mix of history and unshakeable love that I was born, the third and last child to my parents. Dad always joked that he refused to put a ring on my mother's finger until she learned to cook like his mother and aunts and he liked to take full credit for having created the accomplished cook that she became. However, in spite of Dad's claim, the truth is that Mum learned to cook for herself: it brought great comfort to her; she missed her home, her mother and her siblings and food was a reminder of what she held dear.

So, every night I ate a fusion of food that represented the melting pot of cultures that made up my family, steeped in the diverse flavours of the Caribbean.

In my twenties, just as my mother had before me, I began to cook to reminisce and to heal. Somehow, the ritual of cooking and serving became a profound expression of who I am. It also enabled me to have a deeper understanding of my rich culinary heritage.

The Pepperpot Club is a collection of
Caribbean recipes from the land of six races
and many rivers inspired by the wonderful
women in my family who have cooked delicious
food for me throughout my life.

Soups and Favourite Appetisers

Pumpkin Soup

1 tablespoon groundnut oil

2 tablespoon butter

450 g (1 lb) pumpkin (squash),
    peeled and chopped into chunks

1 small onion, grated

2 garlic cloves, crushed

60 g (2 oz) fresh ginger, minced

1 litre (1¾ pints/4¼ cups)
    chicken stock

2 bay leaves

½ teaspoon dried thyme

½ teaspoon dried oregano

½ teaspoon sweet paprika

240 ml (8½ fl oz/1 cup)
    coconut milk

½ teaspoon West Indian
    pepper sauce

double cream and pinches
    of cayenne pepper, to garnish

sea salt and freshly ground
    black pepper, to taste

Heat the oil in a saucepan over a medium heat. Add the butter and stir until it has melted. Toss in the chunks of pumpkin, stir until coated with the oil and butter and add 2 tablespoons of water. Cover the pan with a lid and leave to sweat for a few minutes until the pumpkin has softened slightly. Gently crush with a fork and then add the onion, garlic and ginger.

Add the stock, bay leaves, thyme, oregano, paprika and coconut milk and stir well. Put the cover back on the pan, reduce the heat and simmer for about 15 minutes until the pumpkin is tender.

Remove the bay leaves and purée half of the soup with a hand-held blender or in a food processor. Return the puréed soup to the pan with the remaining unpuréed soup, add the pepper sauce and season well. Garnish with a swirl of double cream and a pinch of cayenne pepper. Serve in warmed bowls, with slices of crusty bread.

Callaloo Soup

My recipe is inspired by my friend Sherwin Paul's mum, Aunty Babse. He misses his mum's cooking and says his favourite of all her dishes is Callaloo soup. It is delicious and I have tried to make it look more appetizing by using cooked white crab meat as opposed to having to suck it out of some ugly hairy crab!

SERVES *6*

500 g (1 lb 2 oz) baby spinach,
    stems removed and
    leaves chopped
1.5 litres (2½ pints/6¼ cups)
    chicken stock
1 onion, chopped
3 garlic cloves, crushed
4 spring onions (scallions), chopped
125 g (4 oz) pancetta, cubed
125 g (4 oz) stewing beef, cut
    into bite-sized pieces
1 teaspoon dried thyme
120 ml (4 fl oz) coconut milk
250 g (9 oz) okra, sliced
250 g (9 oz) cooked white crab meat
1 teaspoon West Indian
    pepper sauce
finely chopped coriander
    (cilantro) leaves, to garnish
salt and freshly ground black
    pepper, to taste

In a large saucepan, cover the spinach with the stock and add the onion, garlic, spring onions, pancetta, beef and thyme. Bring to the boil, then reduce the heat, cover the pan with a lid and simmer for about 45 minutes until the meat is tender.

Add the coconut milk and okra and continue to simmer for a further 10 minutes.

Add the crab meat and season with salt, pepper and pepper sauce. Simmer for a further 5 minutes, garnish with the coriander and serve in warmed bowls.

I remember being forced to
try this soup in 1974. I hated
the look of it and was scared
by the crabs looking out at
me. but I grew to love it.

Chicken and Sweetcorn Soup

I hate to say this but I have always enjoyed corn soup more in the Caribbean than in the UK. It is very popular in Trinidad and Jamaica. In British restaurants there is a tendency to thicken the broth too much and I find it gloopy and cloying. I make it like my mum taught me and the result is a much lighter, satisfying dish. You can substitute the chicken for crab meat, should you prefer.

SERVES **6**

Pour the stock into a saucepan and stir in the creamed corn. Season generously, then add the light soy sauce and pepper sauce. Over a medium heat, gently bring to the boil.

Reduce the heat and slowly pour in the beaten eggs, whisking with a fork. Add the shredded chicken and simmer for 5 minutes.

Divide the soup among warmed bowls and garnish with green and red chillies, spring onions and a few drops of soy sauce.

1 litre (1¾ pints/4¼ cups)
    chicken stock
2 x 418 g (15 oz) tin cans
    of creamed corn
2 teaspoons light soy sauce
1 teaspoon West Indian
    pepper sauce
3 eggs, beaten
600 g shredded cooked chicken
finely sliced green and red chillies,
    spring onions (scallions) and
    dark soy sauce, to garnish
salt and freshly ground black
    pepper, to taste

Monday Soup with Dumplings

My mum called this recipe cabbage soup but it is so much more than that, and I thought it sounded off-putting, so I renamed it Monday Soup. She often cooked it on Mondays when she was tired from all the cooking and socialising from the weekends. It is filling, nutritious and very comforting, and sets one up for the week ahead.

SERVES *6*

For the Monday soup

2 tablespoons vegetable oil

1 kg (2 lb 3 oz) stewing beef,
    cut into large chunks

1 onion, cut in half and finely sliced

250 g (9 oz/3⅓ cups) white
    cabbage, shredded

1 litre (1¾ pints/4 cups)
    chicken stock

2 carrots, halved lengthways
    and cut on the bias

4 large tomatoes, peeled and diced

4 potatoes, quartered

4 tablespoons tomato purée

1 tablespoon light soy sauce

2 teaspoons Worcestershire sauce

2 teaspoons dried thyme

½ teaspoon West Indian
    pepper sauce

finely chopped parsley, to garnish

salt and freshly ground
    black pepper

For the dumplings

225 g (8 oz/1¾ cups) plain
    (all-purpose) flour

1 tablespoon caster
    (superfine) sugar

1 tablespoon spring onions
    (scallions), finely sliced

¼ teaspoon freshly ground
    black pepper

Heat the oil in a large saucepan. Brown the beef on all sides, then add the onion and cabbage and continue to fry for about 5 minutes until the cabbage begins to soften.

Pour in the stock and the other vegetables. Then add the tomato purée together with all the remaining soup ingredients, except for the chopped parsley, and season to taste. Bring to the boil, then reduce the heat, cover with a lid and simmer for about 1 hour until the meat is tender and the potatoes are cooked through.

To make the dumplings, put the flour in a mixing bowl and add the sugar, spring onions and black pepper. Slowly add enough water to form a soft dough that is runny but not too dense.

Before serving the soup, remove the lid and reduce the soup to your desired consistency. Meanwhile, using a teaspoon, scoop up a ball of the dumpling dough and mould it with a second teaspoon. Repeat until all the dough has been used. Drop the dumplings into the soup and simmer for about 5 minutes until cooked through.

Divide the soup among warmed bowls, making sure that each one has some beef, vegetables, potatoes and dumplings. Garnish with the parsley.

I have t
must s
him to
too mu
afraid
heckle
what he
come
I am
home
up on
& con
While
does w
I am
home.
At hom
there a
yes, b
waiting
you o
holida

...confidence in him, + he
... If he needs anything let
...rite me, + rest a lot. You
...rest + go out less. Roy I'm
...you may be spending too much
...by, take think of your age +
... you done, keep from wicked
... + regard your health as first
...mother + I know what
...are like, take my advice
...an be ~~you~~ a better friend
...union than your mother.
...me often + see that they
...get into bad company.
...unting the days to back
... is nice to so as
...in a foreign ... e
...no children ... you
...not when my babes ...
...or me. I appreciate all that
...son, but I am just as longing

Crabback Cakes

Crabbacks are one of Guyana's best contributions to our world and one of their national dishes. Due to its humid muddy terrain, Guyana's mud flats are home to an abundant variety of crabs. Traditionally the crab meat stuffing is made and then placed in crabback shells and baked until brown. My version combines the right flavours with ease.

MAKES *8*

2 eggs

2 tablespoons mayonnaise

1 tablespoons Dijon mustard

1 teaspoon West Indian hot
   pepper sauce

2 tablespoons Worcestershire sauce

1 tablespoon finely sliced spring
   onions (scallion)

1 red onion grated

450 g (1 lb) cooked white crab meat

4 tablespoons breadcrumbs

pinch of cayenne pepper

60 g (2 oz/½ cup) plain
   (all-purpose) flour

2–3 tablespoons vegetable oil

30 g (1 oz) salted butter

finely chopped parsley, to garnish
   and lemon wedges, to serve

salt and freshly ground black
   pepper, to taste

Lightly beat the eggs in a large mixing bowl. Add the mayonnaise, mustard, pepper sauce, Worcestershire sauce, spring onions, red onion, crab meat and breadcrumbs and stir with a fork or use your hands until the ingredients are well combined. Add a large pinch of cayenne pepper and season generously.

Spread the flour on a flat plate. Form the crab mixture into 8 patties, then dip them into the flour and coat evenly on both sides. Cover and set aside in the refrigerator until you are ready to cook (minimum of 30 minutes).

Heat two frying pans over a medium heat each containing 1 tablespoon of the vegetable oil and half of the butter. When the butter has melted and starts to foam, fry the patties for 3–4 minutes until they are golden brown on each side, turning once. Garnish with sprinkles of finely chopped parsley, and serve with lemon wedges and a Salmon Tartar (see page 156).

Coconut Shrimp

I absolutely love these and can devour trays of them. They make great canapés for a cocktail party, although I have also been known to happily eat a mountain of them in front of the TV!

SERVES *4-6*

Preheat the oven to 190°C (375°F/Gas 5). Grease a baking tray with a light coating of vegetable or groundnut oil and place it in the oven on a high shelf for at least 15 minutes while you prepare the prawns.

Rinse the prawns and pat dry on kitchen paper. Place them in a shallow dish, then pour over half the lime juice, season generously and sprinkle over the garlic powder, paprika and cayenne pepper.

Put the cornflour and desiccated coconut into two separate bowls. In the third bowl, whisk the egg whites to soft peaks. Take the preheated baking tray out of the oven.

Dredge the prawns individually in the cornflour (shaking off any excess flour), then dip them in the egg whites and finally dip in the coconut. Lay the prawns in rows on the baking tray, making sure that there is space between each one, and drizzle with a light coating of oil.

Bake for about 20 minutes, turning once after 10 minutes, until the prawns are cooked through and golden brown. Garnish with the parsley, sprinkle over the remaining lime juice and serve.

24 large raw prawns, shelled and
    deveined but with tails left on
juice of 1 lime
½ teaspoon garlic powder
½ teaspoon sweet paprika
large pinch of cayenne pepper
40 g (1½ oz/⅓ cup)
    cornflour (cornstarch)
175 g (6 oz/2 cups)
    desiccated coconut
3 egg whites
vegetable or groundnut oil, to coat
finely chopped parsley, to garnish
salt and freshly ground
    black pepper

Salt Fish Balls

I could eat these bite-sized balls of gorgeousness until the cows come home. In fact, I find cooking them is a nightmare, as I just can't resist eating them as fast as I fry them!

MAKES APPROXIMATELY *12* BALLS

125 g (4½ oz) salt fish fillet

225 g (8 oz) cold mashed potato

1 small onion, finely diced

1 tablespoon spring onions
    (scallions), finely sliced

1 tablespoon parsley, finely chopped

1 large egg

1 teaspoon West Indian
    pepper sauce

½ teaspoon of Worcestershire sauce

½ teaspoon of light soy sauce

1 teaspoon garlic powder

1 teaspoon English mustard powder

plain (all-purpose) flour, enough to
    shape the balls

groundnut oil, for frying

salt and freshly ground
    black pepper

lime wedges, to serve

red pepper mayonnaise, to serve

To prepare the salt fish, soak it in a bowl of water for 24 hours, changing the water five or six times. Transfer the soaked fish to a saucepan, cover with water and then bring to the boil. Reduce the heat and simmer for about 10 minutes until the fish is tender. Drain the fish, leave it to cool and then flake.

Add the fish to the mashed potato in a large mixing bowl and stir together well. Then add all the remaining ingredients, except for the groundnut oil, and check for seasoning. The mixture should be fairly stiff, yet workable.

With floured hands, shape the mixture into about 12 balls. Heat the oil in a deep saucepan over a medium heat until it is hot, then shallow fry the balls in batches for about a minute on each side or until they are golden brown. Serve with lime wedges, mayonnaise and a tomato, red onion and parsley salad.

Salt Fish and Ackee

This delightful, colourful national dish of Jamaica makes a great breakfast served with Bakes (page 198). The delicate texture of the mild ackees resembles scrambled eggs and creates the perfect balance to the strong flavour of the dried cod.

SERVES 4–6

To prepare the salt fish, soak it in a bowl of water for 24 hours, changing the water five or six times. Transfer the soaked fish to a saucepan, cover with water and then bring to the boil. Reduce the heat and simmer for about 10 minutes until the fish is tender. Drain the fish, leave it to cool and then flake.

Heat the oil in a large frying pan over a medium heat. Add the onion, garlic and red and green peppers and sauté for about 5 minutes until softened. Add the tomatoes, spring onions, thyme, Scotch bonnet chilli and the sugar and continue to cook for a further 5 minutes, until hot through, stirring often.

Add the salt fish and season with salt, pepper and the pepper sauce. Then add the ackee (being careful not to break them as they are very delicate) and the Worcestershire and soy sauces. Serve in warmed bowls.

450 g (1 lb) salt fish, soaked, drained and flaked
2 tablespoons vegetable oil
1 onion, finely sliced
2 garlic cloves
½ red pepper (bell pepper), diced
½ green pepper (bell pepper) diced
2 tomatoes, chopped
2 spring onions (scallions), sliced
1 teaspoon thyme, finely chopped
½ Scotch bonnet chilli, seeded and finely sliced
1 teaspoon demerara sugar
1 teaspoon West Indian pepper sauce
1 x 540 g (19 oz) tin can of ackee
½ teaspoon Worcestershire sauce
½ teaspoon light soy sauce
salt and freshly ground black pepper

My parents' courtship was the stuff of
legend in Georgetown, and is remembered
by a whole generation to this day.

Guyanese people are made up of the six races of the Caribbean: East Indian, Chinese, Mixed European Creole, mostly British and Portuguese, African, North American and indigenous Amerindian.

BBQ Chicken Wings

I adore chicken wings as the meat around the little bones is so flavourful and tender. I never waste the crispy tips either! These delights are best serves as a canapé or as starter with coleslaw. However, they are also great as a midweek family meal served with Cook-up Rice (see page 168), or a baked potato .

SERVES 4-6

Lay the wings out in a baking dish, rub them all over with oil and season generously.

Combine all the remaining ingredients in a mixing bowl and mix thoroughly. Pour the sauce over the wings, cover and leave to marinate in the refrigerator for at least 2 hours.

Preheat the oven to 190°C (375°F/Gas 5). Remove the chicken wings from the refrigerator, uncover and bake for about 20 minutes until the wings are golden and crispy. Serve on warmed plates and serve with fried rice or baked potatoes.

900 g (2 lb) chicken wings

1 tablespoon olive oil

3 garlic cloves, crushed

6 tablespoons tomato ketchup

2 tablespoons light soy sauce

2 tablespoons sherry, dark rum
    or rice wine

2 tablespoons American mustard

2 tablespoons Worcestershire sauce

2 tablespoons demerara sugar

2 tablespoons runny honey

1 teaspoon West Indian
    pepper sauce

salt and freshly ground
    black pepper

My favourite of all the regular visitors to our semi-detached suburban castle in Worton Way, was Mum's old school friend, Cecile. She visited us every year, and continued to do so even after Mum had passed away and up until the end of her own life, eight years later.

Like Mum, Cecile had fallen in love with a 'Roy', only hers was a handsome Scottish engineer who worked in the Caribbean for an oil company. However, the Roys took their brides on two very different life journeys and the best friends became separated by many oceans and two continents. While Mum set up home in London, Cecile willingly travelled around the world with her Roy and they spent a few years in Cornwall. Little did she know that those short years would be the happiest of all her married life. She prayed that they would settle permanently in the UK with her young family, surrounded by friends that she loved.

However, Roy was made redundant and after a fruitless search for work in the UK had no choice but to accept a job in Perth, Western Australia, on the back of the mining boom, in 1969. Suburban Australia in those days was not welcoming to mixed-race outsiders. Cecile's olive skin, sparkling grey eyes and wild-haired exotic beauty made her the target of racism. Most locals presumed that Cecile was part Aboriginal and, in their unsophisticated eyes, deemed her uneducated, untrustworthy and socially undesirable. In grocery stores and at her children's school gates, the other parents ignored her as is if she were nothing more than a lowly domestic help.

Cecile held her head high and struggled to adapt, which she did for her children's sake and to keep the peace within her marriage. She felt alone living in such an isolated city and hated having to conform to the conservatism of that era. She wondered why her husband had landed her in this predicament, and longed for the carefree happiness she had known growing up in the 'Garden City of The Caribbean'. She craved the company of her friends from St Rose's Convent, her siblings and her beloved parents, Bertie and Violet.

Eventually, Cecile resigned herself to her new life and made the most of her situation In time she made firm, life-long friends and as her suburban neighbourhood grew, so did the population of other Caribbean immigrants. She was thankful to have Trinidadians living up the street who understood her, her culture and adored her aromatic, tasty food. Dishes were regularly exchanged and compared and before long the whole street wished to be invited to sample Cecile's superb cooking food.

Like Mum, Cecile taught herself how to cook as a tribute to the life that she had left behind and in recognition of those she loved and missed so deeply. Throughout their lives, the two women used the rituals of preparing food, laying the table and sharing their creations with others as an expression of the secrets that lay within their hearts. These profound emotions were explicable to those of us who truly loved them and who mourn their loss to this day.

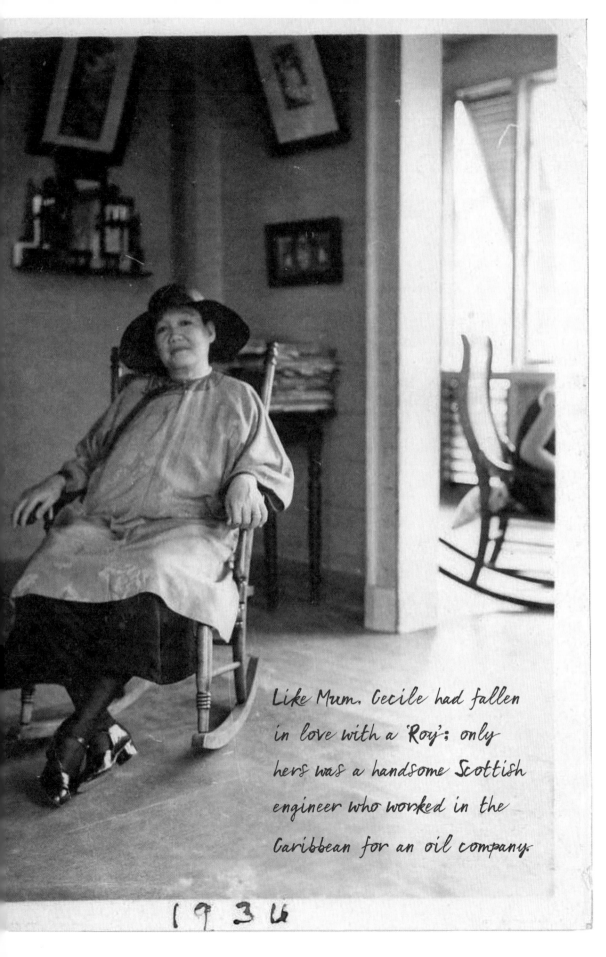

Like Mum. Cecile had fallen
in love with a 'Roy': only
hers was a handsome Scottish
engineer who worked in the
Caribbean for an oil company.

1936

The girls of St Rose's travelled far and wide but in their hearts, they were never far apart.

In her latter years, Cecile developed heart disease and was advised to eat a healthier diet. She did her very best to eat steamed fish and vegetables, but in reality bland food drove her to fever pitch and it took very little prompting for her to sneak into her kitchen and whip up her favourite dishes like curry, fried chicken and sweet 'n' sour spare ribs.

As widows, Mum and Cecile spent hours chatting on the phone, usually on Sundays. They laughed like schoolgirls as they gossiped about their mutual friends, expressed their woes about their children and shared their feelings about getting older. They excitedly planned their next trip when they would be reunited, discussed what they would wear and how much weight they needed to lose in order to eat what they wanted while away. The two friends travelled around the world together and shared many unexpected experiences. The stories of these adventures kept them awake most of the night as they laughed and relished every moment of each other's company.

They also brought out the worst in each other and argued with an intensity common to siblings and people who genuinely love one another. Their lives had started out so alike but became so different; and when questioned about the choices they had made during their marriages, migration and as mothers, they were both convinced that the ways they had chosen were the best and only ways to be. However, beneath the camaraderie and mutual love, they were sure that, had they lived closer to one another, they might have been spared the deep heartbreak and pain that their separation caused.

Cecile's last visit to London to see Mum was in March 2002. Cecile had to take it easy because she was suffering with heart problems and Mum was ill with pemphigus vulgaris, something that few had heard of or understood and, because of this, her illness was often overlooked. This was understandable – she looked so well and healthy. We were hopeful, and slightly in denial, about the seriousness of her condition. No one imagined these two feisty, vital women could ever weaken.

The trip was as social and fun as always, yet tarnished by Cecile witnessing the dreadful pain that my mother was in, particularly at night and with the added strain of the two women hiding the truth from everybody.

As we waved goodbye to Cecile at Heathrow Airport, I stood with my arm around my mum's shoulders, both of us speechless. At that point, I was overcome with a feeling that the two friends were not going to see each other ever again and it dawned on me for the first time that my mother might also die before her time. We drove home in silence, both of us staring out of the windows of the taxi, fighting back tears. We hoped that neither of us would notice the pain in each others' faces.

Mum died on 17 October that same year. Cecile made the long journey back to London as soon as she heard the devastating news. She didn't get to say goodbye to Mum in hospital, but was by our side as my siblings, aunt, uncles and I prepared Mum for her final resting place. Cecile talked to her, stroked her hair tenderly and kissed her dear friend goodbye for the last time.

Cecile remained a good friend to my brother, sister and me. Like Mum, I adopted the habit calling Cecile on Sundays to give her all of our news. She always ended the conversations by exclaiming, 'I love you! I love you! Look after your brother and sister! I love you all!'

As we waved goodbye
to Cecile at Heathrow
Airport, I stood with my
arm around my mum's
shoulders, both of us
speechless.

I visited Perth in 2006 and understood exactly why Cecile had felt so cut off. Even though the city had grown and become more modern, it still retained a feeling of remote isolation. However, Cecile and I cooked happily together and made West Indian meals for her children and grandchildren. We also looked at old photos and found a lovely picture that I had taken of her and Mum on one of our holidays in Malaysia. Both ladies looked radiant and in their prime. After admiring the photograph, she turned to me, grasped my hand and looked me straight in the eye. 'It's time for you to have this,' she whispered. I grinned tenderly, looked deeply into her beautiful, bright eyes and accepted her gift without protest or question. On leaving Perth, I cried all the way from the departure gate to Bangkok, convinced that I was never going to see Cecile again.

Against doctor's orders, Cecile came to see us one more time in 2008. She travelled with her beloved son, Louis, and daughter-in-law, Bronwyn. We had a fabulous couple of weeks spending precious time together. We laughed, gossiped and boy, did we eat! I threw a party in Cecile's honour so she could see all of her old friends, many from her class at St Rose's Convent. I hired a pianist and together we sang songs by Cole Porter, Irving Berlin and Jerome Kern.

We smiled and cried at the memory of the poignant songs and longed for a bygone era of seemingly carefree happiness when we were certain that we'd all see one another again. I then asked for the girls from St Rose's to stand in front of the piano and sing their school song 'Serviam'. Without any prompting (the ladies were now all in their seventies), each girl stood in a circle, held hands and sang their school anthem with clarity, pride and vigour. They sang for themselves, for each other and for the lives that they had left behind in the West Indies; and for their dearly departed friends and family. The girls sang with all their hearts, for probably the last time together, in recognition of where they were from and with an understanding of how far they had come. Hopes and dreams aside, these brave women had lived, loved and embraced life with grace and acceptance.

One day when we were on our own, I asked Cecile what she would request as her last meal if she were on death row. With a wry smile she replied, 'Chinese crispy pork belly!' She told me how she missed it and explained that her doctors and children no longer allowed her to eat it. So without hesitation, I created the recipe on page 56 for my friend based, on the Cantonese sui yuk. Like naughty children, we prepared the pungent, tender pork and waited patiently as the outsized strip of pork slowly roasted and sizzled. The aroma of the marinade, mixed with the sound of the popping crackling of the skin, was so enticing that we had to go out for a walk in order to stop ourselves pulling bits of meat off the joint while it was still cooking in the oven.

Eventually, the magnificent roast was ready and rested. Like rabid beasts Cecile and I hacked into the pork, fat splattering over our faces and dripping down our chins. We nearly broke our teeth as we crunched our way through layers of crispy salty crackling before sinking into mousse-like fat and tender, melt-in-your-mouth, slow-cooked meat. This was our special moment, our secret and our last goodbye.

Cecile died peacefully one Saturday night at home in her own bed after having dinner with her children and grandchildren. Although the comforting sounds of the two women's intimate familiarity echo inside of me, the silence, now they've gone, is deafening.

Storm or cloud will not dismay us,
We will do and dare
When it's dark we'll just remember
That the stars are there
If we fail we'll rise unconquered;
Set our armour right;
Hope and Love will heal our bruises
Faith will win the fight.

Serviam shall be our watchword.
Marching on we'll sing
Battling against the pride of Satan
Serving Christ our King.

2 Supper-time Classics

Crispy Slow Roast Pork Belly

I created this recipe for my beloved friend Cecile. This was her absolute favourite meal, which we cooked together at her request. The aroma of the spicy-sweet marinade is mouth watering, and the sound of the popping crackling will make this dish very hard to resist! Serve with steamed bok choi (or other greens) and rice.

SERVES *6-8*

2 kg (4 lb 6 oz) pork belly, skin scored diagonally and the pork scored into 5 cm (2 in) wide strips

2 tablespoons sherry, rice wine or dark rum

1 tablespoon yellow bean paste

3 cubes fermented bean curd

1 tablespoon hoisin sauce

1 teaspoon five-spice powder

2 tablespoons dark soy sauce

2 garlic cloves, crushed

2 teaspoons grated fresh ginger

1 teaspoon garlic powder

3 tablespoons granulated sugar

2 teaspoons West Indian pepper sauce

salt and freshly ground black pepper

Cut slashes randomly into the underside of the meat about 2.5 cm (1 in) apart. Then place on a plate covered with kitchen paper, dry the top of the skin and leave the meat uncovered in the refrigerator overnight.

To marinate the pork, combine all the remaining ingredients into a smooth paste, season, and pour into a shallow baking tray. Carefully place the pork on top, skin-side up. The meat should be submerged to halfway, with the skin raised above it making sure that none of the marinade touches the skin. Place the tray (uncovered) in the refrigerator for at least 2 hours.

When you are ready to cook, preheat the oven to 240°C (475°F/Gas 9). Take the pork out of the fridge and set it aside until it has reached room temperature. Keep drying the meat during this time. Transfer the meat on to a grill rack over the marinade in the baking tray. Cover generously with salt and then place the baking tray on the top shelf of the oven and cook for 25 minutes, turning the tray once halfway through.

Reduce the oven temperature to 180°C (350°F/Gas 4) and continue to roast for 45 minutes, again turning once halfway through to ensure the meat is cooked evenly. Check the marinade isn't burning, adding a little water to the baking tray, if necessary. Remove the pork from the baking tray and leave it to rest, uncovered, in a warm place for at least 15 minutes. Cut the meat into large cubes with a meat cleaver and serve.

Jerk Chicken

I never tire of this Jamaican classic. In a perfect world, it should be cooked on a barbeque, in a Caribbean beach, while watching the sun go down. However, I promise you that the following recipe tastes almost as good on a cold, wet evening served direct from the oven.

SERVES

Place the chicken in a dish. Make two slashes in the middle of each portion, then rub with a little oil, season and pour over the lime juice.

Place all the remaining ingredients in a food processor and pulse until puréed. Pour the marinade over the chicken and rub all over until the legs are well coated. Cover and refrigerate for at least 2 hours, but preferably overnight.

When you are ready to cook, preheat the oven to 180°C (350°F/Gas 4). Put the chicken on a grill rack in a baking tray together with any remaining marinade and place on the middle shelf of the oven. Bake for 40–50 minutes until cooked through, basting regularly. Serve with a crisp salad of white and red cabbage and carrot, or coleslaw.

6 chicken legs

1 tablespoon groundnut oil

juice of 2 limes

1 large onion, chopped

3 garlic cloves

handful of chopped spring
    onions (scallions)

1 tablespoon chopped thyme

2 Scotch bonnet chillies, halved,
    seeded and finely sliced

5 cm (2 in) piece of fresh
    ginger, chopped

3 tablespoons ground allspice

3 tablespoons white wine vinegar

2 tablespoons demerara sugar

2 tablespoons dark soy sauce

2 tablespoons dark rum

salt and freshly ground
    black pepper

Pepperpot

This national dish of Guyana is not the prettiest of dishes, but it is certainly one of the tastiest. The key ingredient, casereep, is made from cassava root, and adds flavour as well as a dark brown colour. We always ate this dish for breakfast on Christmas morning with Jamaican hard dough bread for dipping in the gorgeous dark and gelatinous gravy.

SERVES *6-8*

2–3 tablespoons groundnut oil

450 g (1 lb) pork shoulder chops, cut into bite-sized pieces

450 g (1 lb) stewing beef, cut into bite-sized pieces

3 pigs trotters, chopped into large chunks

150 ml (5 fl oz/⅔ cup) casereep

1 large cinnamon stick, broken in half

4 tablespoons sugar

2 teaspoons West Indian pepper sauce

2 Scotch bonnet chillies, halved, seeded and finely sliced, plus extra to garnish

12 cloves

salt and freshly ground black pepper

Heat the groundnut oil in a large saucepan over a medium heat and brown the pork, beef and trotters on all sides, in batches if necessary. Return all the meat to the saucepan and season. Add enough water and cover with a lid, bring to the boil, then reduce the heat and simmer for 1 hour.

Add all the remaining ingredients and bring back to the boil. Then reduce the heat again and simmer for about 2 hours until the meat is tender and the gravy is thick, dark and glossy. Garnish with a red Scotch bonnet, and serve on warmed plates with bread or rice.

Temperaments and meals
were cross-cultural,
diverse and, in some
ways, incongruous.

Creole Chicken

The flavours and colours of this hearty, spicy chicken casserole reflect everything that is good about the Caribbean and it is satisfying on any occasion. In my opinion, any stew tastes even better the next day, so make sure that you make plenty for leftovers.

SERVES *4–6*

4 tablespoons groundnut oil
   or light olive oil
8 chicken pieces
50 g (2 oz/scant ½ cup) plain
   (all-purpose) flour
1 large red onion, thinly sliced
2 celery sticks, sliced
½ green pepper (bell pepper),
   halved, seeded and diced
½ red pepper (bell pepper), halved,
   seeded and diced
½ yellow pepper (bell pepper),
   halved, seeded and diced
3 garlic cloves, crushed
2 birdseye chillies, halved, seeded
   and finely sliced
1 Scotch bonnet chilli, halved,
   seeded and finely sliced
3 sprigs of fresh thyme or
   1 teaspoon dried thyme
1 teaspoon dried oregano
2 bay leaves
1 x 400 g (14 oz) tin can of
   chopped tomatoes
350 ml (11 fl oz/1⅓ cups)
   chicken stock
salt and freshly ground
   black pepper

Heat the oil in large heavy casserole dish over a medium heat and sauté the chicken pieces until brown on all sides. Remove the chicken and set aside, leaving the oil and chicken juices in the dish.

Make a roux by adding the flour to the oil and stirring it constantly until the flour begins to brown. Add the onion, celery, peppers, garlic and both types of chilli and cook for a few minutes until the vegetables are well coated and beginning to soften. Add the thyme, oregano, bay leaves and tomatoes, then pour in the stock and stir well.

Return the chicken pieces to the casserole dish, cover and simmer for 45 minutes. Remove the lid, taste and season. If the gravy is too thin, keep simmering with the lid off to thicken, or if it is too thick, add some water or chicken stock to thin it out.

Serve on warmed plates with Vegetable Yellow Rice (see page 160) or Sweet Potato and Yam Gratin (see page 171).

Spiced Baked Chicken

This recipe works equally well with pork loin chops and shoulder steaks.

Preheat the oven to 220°C (425°F/Gas 7). Spread the chicken on a baking dish, cover and leave until they are at room temperature. Remove the cover and drizzle the oil over the fillets, then sprinkle over each of the remaining ingredients and combine them by rubbing together with both hands.

Separate the fillets and add 2 tablespoons of water to the dish. Cover the baking dish with foil and place on a high shelf in the oven and bake for 15 minutes. Then remove the foil, reduce the temperature to 190°C (375°F/Gas 4) and return the dish to the oven for a further 10 minutes (turning halfway through), or until the chicken is a rich golden brown.

Serve the chicken on a bed of Thai fragrant rice, steamed vegetables and the juices from the baking tray.

6 chicken thigh fillets

1 tablespoon groundnut oil

1 tablespoon light soy sauce

1 teaspoon West Indian
  pepper sauce

1 teaspoon garlic powder

2 pinches of five-spice powder

Stewed Chicken

Rich in flavour and colour, this is the perfect one-pot meal for family suppers or dinner parties and will never fail to impress.

2 kg (4 lb 6 oz) chicken pieces

2 tablespoons groundnut oil

2 tablespoons brown sugar

50 g (2 oz/scant ¼ cup)
    creamed coconut

2 tablespoons tomato purée

2 tomatoes, chopped

800 ml (27 fl oz/3¼ cups) chicken stock

For the marinade

juice of 1 lime

2 teaspoons clear malt vinegar

1 tablespoon dark soy sauce

1 onion, halved and finely sliced

4 garlic cloves, crushed

2 teaspoons finely grated
    fresh ginger

2 Scotch bonnet chillies, halved,
    seeded and finely sliced

2 teaspoons dried thyme

1 teaspoon sweet paprika

1 teaspoon garlic powder

1 teaspoon allspice

1 tablespoon finely chopped parsley

1 tablespoon finely chopped
    coriander (cilantro) leaves,
    plus extra for garnish

2 tablespoons chopped spring
    onions (scallions)

1 red pepper (bell pepper), halved,
    seeded and cut into strips

salt and freshly ground
    black pepper

SERVES *6-8*

To marinate the chicken, place the chicken pieces in a large dish and pour over the lime juice and vinegar. Season well, then add the remaining marinade ingredients. Combine well with your hands, cover and leave to marinate in the refrigerator for 2 hours.

When you are ready to cook, bring the chicken pieces to room temperature and then drain them from the marinade, setting the juices to one side for later use. Heat the oil in a deep heavy saucepan over a medium heat. When the oil is smoking, add the sugar and give it a good stir. When the sugar starts to bubble and caramelise, add the chicken pieces and coat well.

Reduce the heat, add the creamed coconut and stir until combined. Mix in the tomato purée, then cover the pan and simmer for 15 minutes. Remove the lid and stir in the tomatoes, reserved marinade and chicken stock and bring to the boil. Reduce the heat once again and simmer for about 1 hour until the chicken is tender. If the gravy is too thin, keep simmering with the lid off to thicken, or if it is too thick, add some water or chicken stock to thin it out.

Garnish with coriander leaves and serve on warmed plates with a rice of your choice.

Fried Chicken

A Caribbean classic, this dish is best served with a squeeze of fresh lemon juice and a cold glass of beer.

SERVES 8

8 small chicken pieces

juice of 1 lime

2 teaspoons West Indian
    pepper sauce

4 garlic cloves, crushed

2 tablespoons soy sauce

2 teaspoons garlic powder

1 teaspoon onion powder

3 teaspoons sweet paprika

250 g (9 oz/2 cups) plain
    (all-purpose) flour

2 eggs

groundnut or corn oil,
    for frying

salt and freshly ground
    black pepper

Cut two slashes in each of the chicken pieces, then place them in a mixing bowl and pour over the lime juice and pepper sauce. Add the garlic and soy sauce and mix well. Season with salt and pepper and 1 teaspoon of the garlic powder together with the onion powder and 2 teaspoons of the paprika. Cover and leave to marinate for at least 30 minutes.

Divide the flour between two plates. Season one of the plates of flour with the remaining garlic powder and paprika and some salt and pepper. In a bowl, beat the eggs.

When you are ready to cook, heat the oil in a deep heavy saucepan over a medium-high heat. Take each piece of chicken and dredge it in the plain flour then the egg wash and then coat in the seasoned flour. Drop into the oil and fry for about 10 minutes on each side until brown and cooked through. Serve immediately, whilst still hot, with wedges of lemon.

Braised Spice Beef

SERVES *4-6*

1 kg (2 lb 3 oz) stewing beef, cut into
    5 mm (¼ in) thick slices

1 tablespoon chilli powder

2 teaspoons sweet paprika

2 teaspoons garlic powder

2 teaspoons ground cumin

1 teaspoon mixed spice

1 teaspoon ground nutmeg

3 tablespoons groundnut oil,
    plus extra to coat beef

large knob of butter

1 large white onion, thinly sliced
    into rings

1 tablespoon demerara (raw) sugar

1 tablespoon Worcestershire sauce

1 tablespoon light soy sauce

2 teaspoons West Indian
    pepper sauce

2 tablespoons tomato ketchup

100 g (¾ cup) chopped dark
    unsweetened chocolate

400 g (14 oz) tin can of chopped
    tomatoes in juice

600 ml (20 fl oz/2½ cups) beef stock

salt and freshly ground
    black pepper

To marinate the beef, put the beef slices in a large dish. Combine the dry spices and sprinkle them over the beef, covering the slices well on both sides. Season well, cover and leave to marinate in the refrigerator for at least 2 hours, but preferably overnight.

When you are ready to cook, heat 2 tablespoons of the oil in a large frying pan over a medium heat. Brush the beef slices with oil and flash fry on both sides until they are sealed and browed. Remove the beef from the pan and set aside.

Add the remaining oil to the pan together with the butter. When the butter has melted, add the onion rings and cook for about 5 minutes until they are soft and translucent.

Pour in any juices that have collected while the beef is resting and then sprinkle over the sugar and stir until it has dissolved. Add the Worcestershire, soy and pepper sauces together with the tomato ketchup and stir.

Sprinkle over the chocolate pieces and stir gently until they have melted. Pour in the chopped tomatoes and beef stock and bring to the boil. Then return the beef to the pan, reduce the heat, cover and braise for about 1½ hours until the meat is melt-in-your mouth tender. If the gravy is too thin, keep simmering with the lid off to thicken, or if it is too thick, add some water or beef stock to thin it out.

Minced Beef Rissoles

This is another example of how my mother used to make things 'stretch' when things were tight. A little left-over mashed potato, mixed with a few store cupboard ingredients, all spiced up with a little family love. What could be better?

SERVES 4-6

Place all the ingredients, except for the flour, in a mixing bowl and season to taste. Combine by hand thoroughly and then shape the mixture into rissoles using your hands or by using two dessertspoons. Add a little water to the mixture if it is too dense or add a few breadcrumbs if you find it too loose.

Heat some oil in a frying pan over a medium heat. Put the flour into a bowl and dip the rissoles in the flour. Shake off any excess and shallow-fry for about 4 minutes on each side until cooked through. Lift the rissoles out of the pan with a slotted spoon and drain on kitchen paper before serving. Alternatively, preheat the oven to 180°C (350°F/Gas 4). Lightly oil a baking tray and place in the oven to warm through. Place the rissoles on the tray and bake for 20–25 minutes, turning once, until cooked through.

These tasty treats are delicious served as snacks or as a main meal with vegetables and fried rice.

500 g (1 lb 2 oz) minced
  (ground) beef
250 g (9 oz/generous 1 cup)
  cooked mashed potato
1 onion, grated
2 tablespoons finely sliced
  spring onions (scallions)
1 large egg, beaten
1 teaspoon dried mixed herbs
1 tablespoon finely chopped parsley
2 teaspoons garlic powder
1 teaspoon West Indian
  pepper sauce
1 tablespoon light soy sauce
2 teaspoons Worcestershire sauce
3 tablespoons plain
  (all-purpose) flour
vegetable oil, for frying
salt and freshly ground
  black pepper

BBQ Jerk Ribs

This no-fuss recipe take just minutes to prepare and the results are delicious! Sticky, spicy and sweet, these tasty ribs will soon become a firm favourite for all your family and friends!

SERVES 4

Place the ribs in a saucepan, cover with water and bring to the boil. Reduce the heat and simmer, uncovered, for 40 minutes. Drain the ribs and set aside to cool.

To make the jerk seasoning, place all the ingredients in a food processor and pulse into a coarse paste.

Place the ribs in non-metallic dish and pour over the jerk seasoning. Cover and leave to marinate in the refrigerator for at least 2 hours or for up to 24 hours.

When you are ready to cook, preheat the oven to 190°C (375°F/Gas 5). Bring the ribs to room temperature and then place them in a baking tray and roast for 30 minutes, turning once or twice, until they are cooked through and tender.

Meanwhile, make the barbecue sauce. Warm all the ingredients together in a saucepan over a medium heat until the sugar has dissolved, but do not boil.

Brush the ribs with the barbecue sauce and continue to cook for a further 15 minutes, turning and basting every 5 minutes.

900 g (2 lb) pork ribs

For the jerk seasoning

1 onion, diced

2 garlic cloves, crushed

juice of 1 lime

1 tablespoon demerara (raw) sugar

1 teaspoon ground nutmeg

1 teaspoon ground cinnamon

1 teaspoon ground allspice

2 Scotch bonnet chillies, halved, seeded and finely sliced

3 tablespoons dark soy sauce

1 tablespoon white wine vinegar

2 teaspoons sweet chilli sauce

For the barbecue sauce

6 tablespoons tomato ketchup

1 tablespoon dark soy sauce

1 tablespoon Worcestershire sauce

2 tablespoons demerara (raw) sugar

1 teaspoon West Indian pepper sauce

salt and freshly ground black pepper

Somehow, between patients, my mother would tear across the front garden and into our kitchen where she'd pull on an apron and instruct me on what to do with whatever she was cooking for Dad's lunch.

Garlic Pork

This spectacular dish is not for the faint-hearted. Traditionally in the West Indies Garlic Pork is served on Christmas morning for breakfast with a nip of gin to cut through its richness. Mum, true to tradition, only cooked it once a year and we all adored it. The year I left home, I arrived back for Christmas day and smelt the garlic from around the corner way before I even glimpsed our house and I knew I was home. Although a national dish of Guyana, this recipe's roots are Portuguese.

SERVES 4

Put the meat in a large mixing bowl and pour over the lime juice. Season generously and then add the thyme, chillies, cloves and garlic and combine well.

Put the mixture into a 3-litre (5 pint) pickling jar, cover with the vinegar and seal. Leave the jar in cool dark place for five days.

When you are ready to cook, drain the meat and then fry it in hot oil in batches for a few minutes until the pork is golden and crispy. Alternatively, preheat the oven to 190°C (375°F/Gas 5). Lightly oil a baking tray, add the drained pork in an even layer and bake for about 30 minutes, turning once, until cooked through.

Serve on warmed plates with fried white bread and green beans.

1.5 kg (3 lb 5 oz) boneless pork shoulder, cut into large chunks
juice of 2 limes
2 teaspoons dried thyme
3 Scotch bonnet chillies, halved, seeded and finely sliced
12 cloves
10 garlic cloves, finely sliced
850 ml (29 fl oz/3½ cups) distilled white vinegar
oil for frying
salt and freshly ground black pepper

Aunty Ruby's Minchee Pork

Aunty Ruby came to England to keep and eye on all of her nephews and nieces on behalf of her siblings. She was the only one out of her eight siblings to not marry and have babies. At any one time, from the early 1950's through to the late 1970's, Aunty Ruby lived with up to eight of her siblings' children and became a surrogate mother to every one of them. She was a kind, gentle lady who babysat for me in the school holidays and sang me church hymn's whilst cradling me on her knee. In her room, there was a large cabinet where she proudly displayed gifts that her nephews and nieces had bought for the duties that she performed so diligently, in her role as a guardian, mentor and a moral guide. Elaborate, padded chocolate boxes, exotic bottles of liquors and empty perfume bottles took pride of place in her humble abode. Though she never married, Aunt Ruby looked after many children and their children's children. Her memory shines bright and her matriarchal presence is greatly missed. Of all of the dishes that Aunty Ruby served up for so many of my relatives and surrogate children , her Minchee Pork is the dish that she is most remembered for.

SERVES 4

450 g (1 lb) pork belly, cut into 5 cm
    (2 in) wide strips

2 tablespoons groundnut or corn oil

1 onion, finely chopped

2 rashers of smoked back
    bacon, finely sliced

2 garlic cloves, crushed

4 tablespoons shredded
    white cabbage

freshly ground black pepper

3 tablespoons yellow bean paste

few dashes of light soy sauce

½ teaspoon West Indian
    pepper sauce

finely sliced spring onions
    (scallions) to garnish

Put the pork in a saucepan, cover with water and bring to the boil. Reduce the heat, cover and simmer for 20 minutes. Drain the pork, let it cool and then slice into 5 mm (¼ in) wide strips.

Heat the oil in a large frying pan over a medium heat. Add the onion and bacon and sauté for about 5 minutes until the bacon is just cooked through and the onion is soft. Add the garlic and cook for a further 1 minute.

Add the cabbage and combine and then season with the black pepper. Stir in the yellow bean paste and soy sauce. Cover with water and bring to the boil. Reduce the heat, cover with a lid and and simmer for about 25 minutes until the pork is tender.

Just before serving, add the pepper sauce and check for seasoning – the dish should not need salt as the yellow bean paste is very salty. Garnish with the spring onions and serve over white rice with steamed greens.

Great Aunty Ruby, far right, was my grandmother
Amy's sister and my father's aunt.

Harriet's Chicken Rice

This delicious recipe was shared with me by one of my glamorous models from the eighties and great friend, Harriet Close. Harriet is a very accomplished cook, but I insist that she cooks this particular dish for me every time I go to see her, as it's one of my absolute favourite things.

SERVES 4

8 chicken thighs

150 ml (5 fl oz/²/₃ cup) lime juice

5 garlic cloves, crushed

2 chillies, halved, seeded and
  finely sliced

1 teaspoon dried thyme

½ teaspoon ground
  Szechuan peppercorns

2 onions, diced

350 g (12 oz) portobello mushrooms,
  generously sliced

350 g (12 oz) mixed rice
  (wild and long grain)

2 tablespoons sunflower oil

1.25 litres (2 pints/5 cups)
  chicken stock

sea salt, to taste

2 limes, to serve

To marinate the chicken, put the thighs in a large dish. Combine the lime juice, garlic, chillies and dried thyme in a bowl and pour this over the chicken pieces, coating them well on all sides. Season well with salt and pepper and the ground Szechuan peppercorns, cover and leave to marinate in the refrigerator for at least 2 hours, but preferably ovenight.

When you are ready to cook, bring the chicken to room temperature and preheat the oven to 200°C (400°F/Gas 6). Grease a large ovenproof dish and scatter the onions, mushrooms and rice over the bottom. Stir together.

Heat the oil in a frying pan over a medium heat. Drain the chicken from the marinade, setting the marinade to one side for later use. Then fry the chicken for about 10 minutes, turning at least once and until the thighs are evenly browned.

Place the chicken pieces skin side up on top of the rice and pour over the reserved marinade and the chicken stock. Bake in the oven for about 1 hour until all the liquid is absorbed and the chicken thighs are crispy, fragrant and gorgeous. Serve with slices of fresh lime.

Chicken Pelau

SERVES 4

8 chicken pieces

1 large onion, diced

1 large tomato, diced

1 teaspoon dried thyme

2 tablespoons vegetable oil

2 tablespoons granulated sugar

1 tablespoon tomato ketchup

West Indian pepper sauce, to taste

400 g (14 oz/2 cups) rice

150 g (5 oz/1 cup) cubed
    pumpkin (squash)

1 large carrot, diced

400 g (14 oz/1 cup) gungo peas

250 ml (8½ fl oz/1 cup) coconut milk

fresh coriander (cilantro)
    leaves to garnish

For the marinade

juice of 1 lime

1 tablespoon dark rum

1 teaspoon Worcestershire sauce

2 teaspoons dark soy sauce

2 garlic cloves, crushed

1 teaspoon finely grated
    fresh ginger

1 Scotch bonnet chilli, halved,
    seeded and finely sliced

pinch of granulated sugar

dash of olive oil

To marinate the chicken, put the chicken pieces, onion, tomato and thyme in a large dish. Combine the marinade ingredients in a bowl and pour over the chicken, coating the pieces well on all sides. Cover and leave to marinate in the refrigerator for at least 2 hours, but preferably overnight.

When you are ready to cook, heat the oil in a large deep saucepan over a medium heat. Add the sugar and stir, making sure that it doesn't burn. When the sugar becomes dark and bubbling start adding the chicken (with the marinade, onions and tomatoes) and coat in the caramel. Add the ketchup and season with West Indian pepper sauce. Reduce the heat, cover and leave to simmer for 10–15 minutes.

Wash the rice through a sieve several times until the water runs clear and then stir it into the chicken. Add the pumpkin, carrot and peas and give a good stir. Then pour in the coconut milk and 700 ml (24 fl oz/3 cups) of water and bring to the boil. Reduce the heat, cover and simmer for 30–40 minutes until the rice and chicken are tender. Serve on warmed plated and garnish with fresh coriander leaves.

Jamaican-Style Rice and Peas

Hearty and full of flavour, this dish is great served both as a main and a side.

SERVES 4

handful of dried shrimps
   (approximately 8)
1 tablespoon groundnut oil
1 tablespoon ghee or salted butter
1 large red onion
2 garlic cloves
1 Scotch bonnet chilli, halved,
   seeded and finely sliced
2 bay leaves
400 g (14 oz/1 cup)
   green pigeon peas
200 g (7 oz/generous 1 cup)
   easy cook long-grain rice
400 ml (14 fl oz/1³/4 cups)
   coconut milk
300 ml (10 fl oz/1¼ cups)
   chicken stock
1 teaspoon West Indian
   pepper sauce
fresh coriander (cilantro)
   leaves, to garnish
salt and freshly ground
   black pepper

Bring a saucepan of water to the boil and add the dried shrimps. Reduce the heat, simmer for 10 minutes and then drain the shrimps and set aside.

Heat the groundnut oil in a large saucepan over a medium heat. Add the ghee or butter and heat until it has melted. Then add the onion, garlic and chilli and fry for about 5 minutes until soft. Stir in the dried shrimps, bay leaves, peas and rice, and season.

Pour in the coconut milk and stock, then add the pepper sauce and bring to the boil. Reduce the heat, give the contents of the pan a good stir, then cover and simmer for 15–20 minutes until the rice is tender and the liquid is absorbed. Serve in medium-sized bowls, and garnish with coriander leaves.

Coriander is a widely
used herb in Caribbean
cuisine. Fresh, spicey
and aromatic, it is the
perfect garnish to these
firery recipes!

Macaroni and Cheese Pie

SERVES 6 ————————————————————————————————

600 ml (20 fl oz/2½ cups) milk

2 eggs

2 teaspoons English
   mustard powder

1 teaspoon West Indian
   pepper sauce

450 g (1 lb/2½ cups) cooked
   pasta spirals

1 onion, finely chopped

1 teaspoon garlic powder

450 g (1 lb/3²/₃ firmly packed cups)
   mature cheddar, grated

salt and freshly ground
   black pepper

Preheat the oven to 190°C (375°F/Gas 5) and grease a 23 x 33 cm (9 x 13 in) baking dish.

Pour in the milk and beat in the eggs. Season with the mustard powder and pepper sauce together with generous amounts of salt and pepper.

In a bowl, combine the cooked pasta, onion, garlic powder and cheese, leaving a handful of cheese to sprinkle over the top. Add the pasta mixture to the baking dish, sprinkle over the reserved cheese and bake for about 45 minutes until golden brown and firm to the touch.

Caring, sharing, devoted sisters.

Aunty Margaret's Chee-a-tows Macaroni and Cheese

Macaroni and cheese is a major accompaniment in the West Indies and is particularly popular in Barbados, St Lucia, Jamaica and Guyana, where it is served with fried fish, roasts and stews or on its own with a salad. My mother's Macaroni Cheese Pie was delicious and I have based my recipe on hers, (see page 86), which in turn was based on my paternal grandmother Amy Phang's recipe. Mum's beloved sister Aunty Margaret also makes a delicious macaroni and cheese, but in a completely different way to ours. I recommend that you try both of the following recipes and decide which one you prefer. I love them, and their creators, equally.

SERVES 6

Preheat the oven to 180°C (350°F/Gas 4) and butter a large baking dish.

In a saucepan, bring 1 litre (1³/₄ pints/4¼ cups) of water to the boil and add a few drops of oil to stop the pasta from sticking. Add the macaroni, then reduce the heat, cover and leave the pasta to simmer for 6 minutes. Add the onion soup mix and continue to cook for about another 6 minutes until the macaroni is cooked, stirring occasionally to prevent the pasta from sticking. Remove the pan from the heat. Do not drain the macaroni but set it aside.

Place another saucepan over a medium-low heat. Melt the butter, then add the flour and cook, stirring for a minute. Add the milk and whisk together. Take the pan off the heat and add the egg. Return the pan to the heat and stir until the sauce begins to thicken. Add the grated cheese and continue to stir until the cheese melts and is well combined.

Pour the cooked macaroni into the cheese sauce, mix together well and season to taste with pepper. Spoon the macaroni into the prepared baking dish, sprinkle the breadcrumbs over the top and bake for about 20 minutes until the top is golden brown and bubbly. Remove the dish from the oven and let it rest for 5 minutes before serving.

300 g (10½ oz/3¹/₃ cups) elbow macaroni

1 packet of onion soup mix

1 tablespoon salted butter

1 teaspoon plain (all-purpose) flour

300 ml (10 fl oz) milk

1 egg, beaten

400 g (14 oz) mature cheddar cheese, grated

2 tablespoons fresh breadcrumbs

salt and freshly ground black pepper

Oxtail Stew

Oxtail makes a delicious gelatinous glossy gravy and is very popular throughout the Caribbean. Hearty and comforting, this is a perfect winter warmer.

SERVES 4

1 kg (2 lb 3 oz) oxtail, trimmed and
    cut into 5 cm (2 in) chunks
1 tablespoon Caribbean
    green seasoning
2 tablespoons red wine vinegar
2 tablespoons vegetable oil
1 heaped tablespoon brown sugar
1 onion, thinly sliced
3 garlic cloves, finely chopped
2 Scotch bonnet chillies, halved,
    seeded and finely chopped
2 tomatoes, diced
2 celery sticks, sliced at an angle
1 teaspoon light soy sauce
1 teaspoon Worcestershire sauce
½ teaspoon West Indian
    pepper sauce
½ teaspoon dried oregano
½ teaspoon dried thyme
2 tablespoons tomato ketchup
500 ml (17 fl oz/2 cups) beef stock
finely chopped coriander
    (cilantro) to garnish
salt and freshly ground
    black pepper

To marinate the oxtail, place the meat in a large dish. Coat with the green seasoning and pour over the red wine vinegar. Leave to marinate in the refrigerator for at least 2 hours.

Heat the oil in a large saucepan over a medium heat. When it begins to smoke, add the sugar and stir until it is bubbling and a dark caramel colour. Stir in the marinated meat and coat well., then cook for 5 minutes.

Add all the remaining ingredients, except for the coriander leaves, and bring the mixture to the boil. Reduce the heat, cover and simmer for 1½ hours. Remove the lid and continue to simmer for about 30 minutes until the sauce has reduced and is thick and rich.

Garnish with the coriander and serve on warmed plates. Tastes great with Jamaican-style Rice and Peas (see page 84).

So, it was into this heady mix of history and unshakeable love that I was born, the third and last child to my parents. Dad always joked that he refused to put a ring on my mother's finger until she learned to cook like his mother and aunts and he liked to take full credit for having created the accomplished cook that she became.

Rum Punch Ribs

I created this recipe whilst trying to impress some lovely cooks in Barbados. The seasoning is typically Bajan, with its use of spice, pepper sauce and of course rum.

SERVES 4

2 kg (4 lb 6 oz) thick pork ribs,
    skin removed

6 tablespoons brown sugar

90 ml (4 fl oz/¼ cup) molasses

90 ml (4 fl oz ¼ cup) runny honey

170 ml (6 fl oz/³/₄ cup) apple
    cider vinegar

80 ml (3 fl oz/¹/₃ cup)
    Worcestershire sauce, to taste

6 tablespoons dark rum

2 teaspoons West Indian
    pepper sauce

2 teaspoons garlic powder

1 teaspoon ground allspice

8 tablespoons tomato ketchup

1 tablespoon light soy sauce

1 tablespoon vegetable oil,
    plus extra for frying

salt and freshly ground
    black pepper

Bring a large pan of water to the boil. Season with salt and place the ribs in the water. Reduce the heat, cover and simmer gently for 30–40 minutes. Drain well and allow the ribs to cool down a little.

Mix the remaining ingredients in a bowl with 1 tablespoon of the oil. Whisk gently to make sure the sugar has dissolved properly. Then place the cooled ribs in the marinade, coating them well. Leave to marinate in the refrigerator for at least 2 hours, but preferably overnight.

Heat a little vegetable oil in a frying pan on a medium heat. Drain the ribs, reserving the marinade, and fry the ribs, in batches if necessary, on each side for a few minutes until they are browned well. Add a little of the marinade and allow it to reduce. Cook for 5–10 minutes on a gentle heat until the pork has been heated through and you are left with a thickened sticky sauce. Serve on warmed plates with Corn on the Cob (see page 168).

Guyanese Patties

There are Jamaican Patties, Cornish pasties and then there are Guyanese Patties. They clearly derived from the English meat pies but are seasoned in the Caribbean way and so in my opinion the best of the bunch! This traditional recipe uses lard for the pastry mix, but it tastes equally as good using butter.

MAKES **24**

To make the pastry, add salt to the sifted flour and rub together with the butter and lard using your fingertips, adding plenty of air as you work, until they resemble breadcrumbs. Pour the ice-cold water, a little at a time, and combine the mixture until the dough binds together into a ball. Cover with clingfilm and refrigerate for at least 30 minutes.

For the filling, heat the oil and ghee together in a large saucepan over a medium heat. Add the onion and sauté for about 5 minutes until it is soft and translucent. Then add the beef and stir until it is browned all over and cooked through. Pour away any excess fat.

Add the garlic powder, thyme and chilli and sprinkle this over the flour and mix in thoroughly. Add all the remaining ingredients, cover with water and simmer until the vegetables are soft and the gravy is thick.

Preheat the oven to 190°C (375°F/Gas 5). Oil and flour 2 x 12-hole patty pans. Make an egg wash by beating the eggs with the milk. Roll out the pastry on a floured surface to about 5 mm (¼ in) thick and using a 7.5 cm (3 in) diameter pastry cutter cut out about 48 discs. Line the base of the patty pans with half of the pastry discs and fill each disc with 1½–2 teaspoons of the beef filling.

Brush the pastry edges with egg wash and place another disc on top for a lid. Stab each patty on the top with a fork to allow air to escape when they are cooking and brush with some more egg wash. Bake for 20–25 minutes until golden. Allow the patties to cool and serve.

For the shortcrust pastry

450 g (1 lb/3²/₃ cups) plain
    (all-purpose) flour, sifted
2 pinches of salt
115 g (3½ oz/scant ½ cup)
    salted butter, cubed
115 g (3½ oz/scant ½ cup)
    lard, cubed
4–5 tablespoons ice-cold water
2 eggs
2 tablespoons milk

For the filling

1 tablespoon vegetable oil
1 tablespoon ghee
1 onion, finely diced
450 g (1 lb) minced (ground) beef
2 teaspoons garlic powder
1 tablespoon chopped thyme
1 Scotch bonnet chilli, halved,
    seeded and finely sliced
2 teaspoons plain (all-purpose) flour
1 small carrot, finely diced
2 tablespoons frozen peas
2 teaspoons Worcestershire sauce
1 tablespoon light soy sauce
1 tablespoon tomato ketchup
1 teaspoon West Indian peppe sauce
salt and freshly ground
    black pepper

Spiced Beef in a Chocolate Sauce

Serve alongside a warm bowl of Cook up Rice (see page 167).

SERVES 4

For the spiced beef in a
chocolate sauce

2–3 tablespoons vegetable oil

1 large white onion, sliced

1 kg (2 lb 3 oz) stewing beef,
     cut into 1 cm thick medallions

2 teaspoons chilli powder

2 teaspoons sweet paprika

2 teaspoons garlic powder

2 teaspoons ground cumin

1 teaspoon mixed spice

1 teaspoon ground nutmeg

2 tablespoons demerara sugar

4 tablespoons tomato ketchup

1 tablespoon light soy sauce

1 tablespoon Worcestershire sauce

1 teaspoon West Indian
     pepper sauce

400 ml (13 fl oz/1²/₃ cups) beef stock

400 g (14 oz) tin can of chopped
     tomatoes in juice

80 g (3 oz/½ cup) chopped 70%
     dark chocolate

2 tablespoons chopped parsley

For the beef, heat the oil in a large saucepan over a medium heat. Add the sliced onion and sauté for 1 minute. Increase the heat to high, add the beef medallions and brown on each side. Sprinkle over the chilli, sweet paprika, garlic powder, cumin, mixed spice, nutmeg and sugar. Turn the meat frequently to coat each piece of beef in the spices. Allow it to cook for a few minutes until the spices become fragrant.

Add the ketchup with the soy, Worcestershire and pepper sauces. Continue to turn the meat to coat it well. Add the beef stock and tomatoes and season with a little salt and pepper.

Bring the mixture up to the boil, then reduce the heat and bring the mixture down to a gentle simmer. Break the chocolate into the sauce, stir well and place a lid on the pan. Allow it to cook for about 1 hour until the meat has softened and the sauce has thickened.

When the beef is cooked, garnish with the parsley and serve on warmed plates alongside the cook-up rice.

Meatloaf

This is quick to make, economical and very tasty. After a boring day at school I was always thrilled to find this waiting for me. Serve slices of the meatloaf with lashings of buttery mashed potato and baked beans. Leftovers make a great sandwich filling.

SERVES *6-8*

1 tablespoon groundnut oil

1 onion, finely chopped

2 rashers of smoked streaky bacon, finely chopped

450 g (1 lb) minced (ground) beef

450 g (1 lb) minced (ground) pork

2 eggs

500 g (1 lb 2 oz/6¼ cups) fresh breadcrumbs

2 teaspoons garlic powder

2 teaspoons onion powder

4 dashes of Worcestershire sauce

2 teaspoons West Indian pepper sauce

1 tablespoon English mustard

Preheat the oven to 190°C (375°F/Gas 5). Lightly oil a large roasting tin and place it in the centre of the oven to warm through.

Heat the oil in a frying pan over a medium heat. Add the onion and bacon and sauté for about 5 minutes until the bacon is just cooked through and the onion is soft. Set aside and leave to cool.

In a large mixing bowl, combine the beef and pork with the eggs and breadcrumbs. Season with all the remaining ingredients and then add the cooled bacon and onion. Mix well with both hands.

Divide the mixture in half and mould into two loaves side by side on the warmed roasting tin. Roast for about 45 minutes or until the meat juices run clear. Remove from the oven and let the meatloafs rest for 10 minutes before slicing.

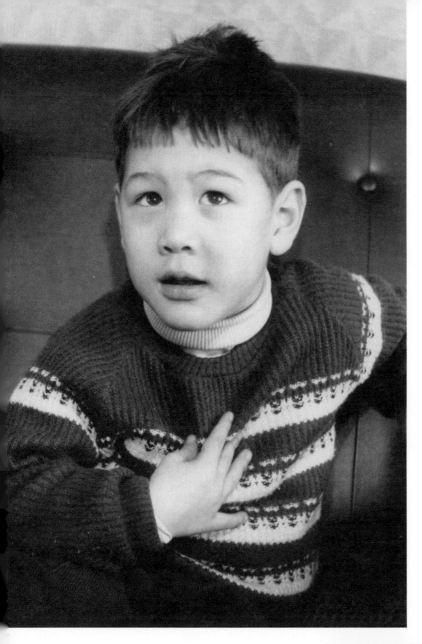

Posey and vying for attention.
Little has changed...

3 Asian Flavours

Caribbean Chicken Curry

This curry has several layers of complex flavours and is bursting with spice – it hasn't caused any upset to those I have served it to so far! It is delicious served with plain jasmine rice and lightly stir-fried vegetables.

SERVES 4-6

2 tablespoons groundnut oil

1 tablespoon ghee or salted butter

6 cardamom pods

8 cloves

2 cinnamon sticks

4 star anise

1 large onion, finely sliced

3–4 garlic cloves, crushed

2 teaspoons grated fresh ginger

2 pinches of granulated sugar

4 tablespoons medium Madras
    curry paste

1 teaspoon five-spice powder

8 chicken thighs

2 dashes of light soy sauce

West Indian pepper sauce, to taste

125 g (4 oz/½ cup) creamed
    coconut, cubed

400 g (14 oz) tin can
    chopped tomatoes

chopped coriander (cilantro)
    leaves to garnish

salt and freshly ground
    black pepper

Heat the oil in a large heavy casserole dish over a medium heat. Add the ghee or butter and heat until it has melted. Then add the cardamom pods, cloves, cinnamon sticks and star anise and sauté for about 5 minutes until the oil is infused with their flavour.

Add the onion, garlic, ginger and a pinch of the sugar and sauté for a further 5 minutes or until the onion begins to caramelise. Then stir in the curry paste and five-spice powder and cook for a few more minutes. Add the chicken and sauté for 2–3 minutes on each side to seal. Pour in 100 ml (3½ fl oz/scant ½ cup) of water, cover and cook for about 15 minutes until the chicken is cooked through.

Remove the lid and season the chicken with the soy and pepper sauces and the second pinch of the sugar. Season with salt and pepper. Add the creamed coconut and stir until it has melted, then add the tomatoes. Simmer until the meat is very tender and the gravy is at your preferred consistency. If the gravy is too thin, keep simmering with the lid off to thicken, or if it is too thick, add some water or chicken stock to thin it out.

Serve on warmed plates with steamed jasmine rice and stir-fried vegetables, garnished with the coriander.

Channa and Spinach Curry

This healthy vegetarian curry is great served with a fresh, warm Roti (see page 180).

SERVES 4-6

Heat the oil in a deep frying pan or saucepan over a medium heat. Add the onion, garlic and chillies and cook for about 5 minutes until soft. Stir in the curry powder and cook for a further 5 minutes, adding a little more oil or water if it starts to burn.

Stir in the potatoes and chickpeas and season with the pepper sauce, tomato ketchup and salt and pepper. Add enough water to just cover and bring to the boil. Then reduce the heat, cover and simmer for 25 minutes, or until the flavours have mixed together and the water is absorbed. Add the spinach and continue to cook for a further 5 minutes. Serve on warmed plates with Roti (see page 180) or as an accompaniment to a meat curry.

1 tablespoon vegetable oil

1 onion, finely sliced

2 garlic cloves, crushed

2 birdseye chillies, halved,
    seeded and finely sliced

2 tablespoons Madras curry powder

2 potatoes, roughly chopped

400 g (14 oz) tin can of chickpeas,
    washed and drained

½ teaspoon West Indian
    pepper sauce

1 teaspoon tomato ketchup

200 g (7 oz/4½ cups)
    shredded spinach

salt and freshly ground
    black pepper

Vegetable Curry

This delicious curry is equally successful served as an accompaniment or as a main meal.

SERVES *6*

½ teaspoon cumin seeds

2 teaspoons ground coriander

2 tablespoons vegetable oil

1 onion, thinly sliced

2 garlic cloves, crushed

1 teaspoon grated fresh ginger

2 chillies, halved, seeded and
    finely sliced

1 teaspoon allspice

2 beef tomatoes, chopped

1 tablespoon medium curry paste

450 g (1 lb) cubed butternut squash

600 ml (20 fl oz/2½ cups) chicken
    or vegetable stock

125 g (4 oz/1²/₃ cups) chopped
    white cabbage

1 plantain, sliced

400 g (14 oz) tin can of chickpeas,
    drained and rinsed

West Indian pepper sauce

1 tablespoon chopped coriander
    (cilantro) leaves

salt and freshly ground
    black pepper

Heat a large frying pan over a low heat and dry sauté the cumin seeds and ground coriander for about 1 minute. Add the oil, onion, garlic, ginger and chillies and sauté for about 5 minutes until soft.

Sprinkle over the allspice and stir in the chopped tomatoes and curry paste. Cook the paste for a few minutes, then add the butternut squash and cook for 5 minutes. Add the stock and bring to the boil before reducing the heat and leaving the curry to simmer for 10 minutes.

Stir in the cabbage and plantain and cook for a further 10 minutes. Add the chickpeas and simmer for 5 minutes before checking for seasoning and adding salt, pepper and the pepper sauce to taste. Garnish with the chopped coriander and serve.

My mother could curry almost anything and make it taste fantastic. I grew up eating curry at least twice a week. Mum's theory (which I agree with wholeheartedly) was to make the curry as simple as possible and without too many complex layers of flavour. She didn't want her dishes, 'fighting up against each other and repeating on people all night!'

Beef and Pork Curry

I love the textural combination of beef and pork in this recipe. However, I would never have thought of it had my mother not opened the wrong parcel of meat one day and threw it in the curry pot without thinking. Happily, we all loved it and it became part of Mum's regular repertoire. My brother, sister and I still snigger every time we eat it. The recipe works equally as well with diced shoulder of lamb or chicken pieces. If using a whole chicken, cut into eight pieces and then follow the method below, but cook it for an hour only, adding the potatoes at the same time as the water.

SERVES 4-6

400 g (14 oz) stewing beef, cut into
    bite-sized pieces

400 g (14 oz) pork shoulder chops,
    cut into bite-sized pieces

4 teaspoons Madras curry powder

1 teaspoon ground cumin

1 teaspoon garam masala

2 teaspoons garlic powder

3 tablespoons vegetable oil

1 large onion, diced

2 garlic cloves, crushed

1 heaped tablespoon Madras
    curry paste

1 teaspoon West Indian
    pepper sauce

1 tablespoon tomato ketchup

1 teaspoon granulated sugar

3 potatoes, cut into large chunks

salt and freshly ground
    black pepper

Place the beef and pork in a large bowl and season with salt and pepper. Add the curry powder, cumin, garam masala and garlic powder. Mix well with your hands and leave to marinate for 1–2 hours. Bring the meat to room temperature before cooking.

Heat the vegetable oil in a large saucepan over a medium heat, add the onion and garlic and sauté for about 5 minutes to soften. Stir in the Madras curry paste and cook it for 5 minutes, stirring all the time.

Add the meat and fry it on all sides to brown. Add the pepper sauce, tomato ketchup and sugar, and continue to stir for about 5 minutes while the meat releases its natural juices. Add just enough water to cover the meat, place the lid on the saucepan and simmer for 1 hour.

Stir in the potato and continue to simmer for a further 1 hour until the meat is tender and the potatoes are soft. If the gravy is too spicy, add more potato, and if it is too thin, keep simmering with the lid off to thicken.

Serve in warmed bowls with Roti (see page 180) or Dahl Puri (see page 183) to dip into the gravy, and plain rice alongside.

Curried Mince

My brother Dominic loves this curried mince served with simple plain long grain rice.
He also believes it to be an effective cure for a hangover.

SERVES 4

2 tablespoons ghee or vegetable oil

1 tablespoon curry powder

1 teaspoon garam masala

1 teaspoon ground coriander

½ teaspoon ground cardamom

2 bay leaves

450 g (1 lb) minced (ground) lamb
    or beef

1 onion, finely sliced

2 garlic cloves, crushed

1 tablespoon grated fresh ginger

2 birdseye chillies, halved, seeded
    and finely sliced

2 tomatoes, chopped

60 g (2 oz/½ cup) frozen peas

finely chopped coriander (cilantro)
    leaves to garnish

finely chopped mint leaves
    to garnish

salt and freshly ground
    black pepper

Gently heat he oil in a deep saucepan or frying pan. Melt the ghee in the oil. When hot, soften the onion and add the garlic ginger and chillies.

Sprinkle in the curry powder, garam-masala, coriander and cardamom and bay leaves, and stir. Cook out for a couple of minutes, being careful not to allow the spices to burn.

Crumble in the mince and stir until the meat is cooked through. Skin off any excess fat. Add the water, tomatoes and tomato ketchup. Bring to boiling point, put a lid on the pan and simmer gently for an hour.

Take the lid off the pan and add the peas, combine well and cook for a further ten minutes. Add more water to the pan if the mince gravy is drying out. Garnish with a sprinkling of finely chopped coriander and mint.

Serve with rice or bread of choice.

Seafood Curry

This delicious, mild curry can be made with any combination of fish and seafood. Firm white fish such as red snapper, monkfish and cod fillets work best, as they are meaty and tend not to flake and break, unlike the more delicate varieties. Combine the fish with prawns (shrimps) and scallops or lobster if you are feeling extravagant. This easy sauce can be made well in advance and reheated.

SERVES 4-6

Heat the oil in a large frying pan over a medium heat. Add the onion and sauté for about 5 minutes until soft, then add the garlic, ginger, peppers and chillies and season with salt and pepper. Continue to cook for 5 minutes, stir in the curry paste and cook gently for a further 5 minutes.

Stir in the coconut milk, cover and bring to the boil, then reduce the heat and simmer for 5 minutes. Add the tomato purée and mango chutney, stir and check for seasoning.

Add the fish and seafood to the sauce and drizzle over the lime juice. Season and simmer for 7–8 minutes until the fish and seafood are cooked to your liking. Serve on warmed plates with a side of raita and mango chutney. Garnish with coriander and wedges of lime.

3 tablespoons groundnut oil

1 large onion, finely diced

3 garlic cloves, crushed

2 teaspoons grated fresh ginger

1 red pepper (bell pepper), halved, seeded and diced

1 yellow pepper (bell pepper), halved, seeded and diced

2 birdseye chillies, halved, seeded and finely sliced

3 tablespoon Madras curry paste

600 ml (20 fl oz/2½cups) coconut milk

1 tablespoon tomato purée

2 tablespoons smooth mango chutney

700 g (1 lb 8 oz) white fish fillets, such as monkfish or red snapper, chopped into bite-sized pieces

450 g (1 lb) tiger prawns (shrimp), shelled and deveined, with tails on

225 g (8 oz) scallops

juice of 2 limes

finely chopped coriander (cilantro) leaves to garnish

salt and freshly ground black pepper

Curried Shrimps

This Phang family favourite is economical, simple to make and deeply satisfying to eat.

SERVES 4

1 tablespoon sunflower oil

2 teaspoons ghee

1 onion, finely chopped

3 garlic cloves, crushed

1 tablespoon Madras curry powder

1 teaspoon ground cumin

1 teaspoon ground coriander

1 teaspoon turmeric

100 g (3½ oz/⅓ cup) creamed
    coconut, cubed

2 dashes of dark soy sauce

2 dashes of Worcestershire sauce

dash of West Indian pepper sauce

2 bay leaves

1 teaspoon dried thyme

1 teaspoon granulated sugar

450 g (1 lb) cooked and peeled
    frozen tiger prawns, defrosted

2 tomatoes, diced

salt and freshly ground
    black pepper

Heat the oil in large saucepan over a medium heat. Add the ghee and heat until it has melted. Then add the onion and sauté for about 4 minutes until soft, then add the garlic and fry for a further 1 minute. Add the curry powder, cumin, ground coriander and turmeric and cook for 3 minutes, stirring continuously and adding a little extra oil or water if necessary.

Stir in the creamed coconut until it has melted. Then add the soy and Worcestershire sauces and keep stirring. Season and then add the pepper sauce, bay leaves, dried thyme and sugar. Cover with 300 ml (10 fl oz/1¼ cups) of water and simmer until the sauce has reduced by one third.

Add the prawns and tomato and simmer gently for 10 minutes. The prawns will shrink and get a little tough and meaty in texture, which is exactly how they need to be for this dish. Serve on warmed plates with Dahl Puri (see page 183) or with strips of 'Buss Up Shirt' (see page 175) and a cucumber salad.

Cou-Cou

Cou-Cou is one of Barbados's national dishes and often served as an accompaniment to fying fish or meat stews. My version is unorthodox, but I think it is more tasty and comforting than the tradional version.

SERVES 4

500 ml (17 fl oz/2 cups) coconut milk

120 ml (4 fl oz/½ cup) chicken stock
   or vegetable stock

12 okra, sliced

1 onion, grated

3 garlic cloves, crushed

1 tablespoon chopped spring
   onions (scallions)

2 birdseye chillies, halved, seeded
   and sliced

½ red pepper (bell pepper),
   seeded and diced

½ teaspoon sweet paprika

½ teaspoon dried thyme

½ teaspoon dried oregano

1 teaspoon West Indian
   pepper sauce

256 g (9 oz/2 cups) cornmeal

2 tablespoons salted butter

coriander (cilantro) or parsley
   leaves, to garnish

salt and freshly ground
   black pepper

Heat the coconut milk and stock in a large saucepan over a medium-low heat. Add the okra slices and cook for about 5 minutes until tender.

Add the onion, garlic, spring onions, chillies, red pepper, paprika, herbs and pepper sauce and stir to mix. Pour in the cornmeal, a little at a time, and stir vigorously, to avoid burning the bottom and lumps forming. Add a little water if it starts to stick to the bottom of the pan.

Keep stirring the sauce over a low heat until nearly all the liquid is absorbed and stiff peaks can be formed. Remove from the heat and stir in 1 tablespoon of the butter.

Grease a bowl with the remaining butter and pour in the mixture. Smooth the top with the back of a spoon, then leave it to stand for 15 minutes before turning it out on to a serving plate. Garnish with coriander or parsley leaves and serve with long grain rice.

'Co-ordinate and accessorise'
One of Mums many mantras!

A proud moment for Great
Uncle Harry and the Bollers.

Aunty Jean looked even lovelier on her wedding day. Georgetown's answer to Elizabeth Taylor in 'Father Of The Bride'. Grandpa Phang must have felt so proud walking her down the aisle.

Char Sui Pork

There is nothing tastier than a mixture of slices of Char Sui Pork and cubes of Crispy Slow Roast Pork (see page 56) served with steamed rice and stir-fried greens. Always make a double portion of this recipe so you can serve it with Chow Mein (see page 131) the next day.

SERVES 6

700 g (1 lb 8 oz) pork belly,
    skin removed

2 teaspoons five-spice powder

4 tablespoons runny honey

2 chunks of fermented bean curd

2 garlic cloves, crushed

3 tablespoons rice wine

2 tablespoons hoisin sauce

1 tablespoon dark soy sauce

2 teaspoons sweet chilli sauce

salt and freshly ground
    black pepper

To marinate the pork, cut the pork belly into 5 cm (2 in) wide strips. Rub them all over with the five-spice powder and season with salt and pepper. Put all the remaining ingredients into a bowl and mix together until smooth. Pour over the pork then cover and leave to marinate in the refrigerator for at least 2 hours, but preferably overnight.

When you are ready to cook, preheat the oven to 160°C (325°F/Gas 4). Transfer the pork to a baking tray and cook in the oven for 1 hour until tender.

To finish off, preheat the grill to hot and grill the pork strips for about 5 minutes or until they are crisp and caramelised. Rest the meat for at least 10 minutes, slice on an angle and serve on warmed plates with steamed jasmine rice and baby bok choy.

Chinese Fried Rice

Substitute the pork and prawn for eggs to make a vegetarian version that tastes just as great. For that Caribbean kick, add a dash of West Indian pepper sauce.

SERVES 4

2 tablespoons corn oil

1 onion, chopped

3 eggs, beaten

125 g (4 oz) finely diced Char Sui
    pork (see page 122)
    or sliced, cooked Chinese
    sausage (lap cheong)

125 g (4 oz) cooked prawns (shrimps)

60 g (2 oz/½ cup) frozen peas

1 birdseye chilli, halved, seeded
    and finely sliced

550 g (1 lb 4 oz/3 cups) cooked and
    cooled white rice

1 teaspoon West Indian
    pepper sauce

light soy sauce, to taste

sliced spring onions (scallions)
    to garnish

salt and freshly ground
    black pepper

Heat the oil in a wok or large frying pan over a medium heat. When the oil starts smoking, reduce the heat, add the onion and fry for about 4 minutes until it is soft.

Pour in the beaten eggs and swirl around the pan as if making an omelette. When the eggs are set, scramble them until firm and beginning to brown. Then one at a time add the pork, prawns, peas and chilli, and stir-fry until they are heated through.

Stir in the cooked rice, season with salt and pepper and sprinkle with the pepper sauce and soy sauce. Garnish with sliced spring onions and serve.

Chinese Ribs

I have never met a West Indian who doesn't appreciate the flavour and joy of sucking on meat bones and I am no exception. I adore ribs of any description and will undoubtedly spend the rest of my days trying to concoct the perfect recipe. Here is one of my best endeavours to date.

SERVES 4

Place the ribs in a saucepan, cover with water and bring to the boil. Then reduce the heat and simmer, uncovered, for 40 minutes. Drain the ribs and set aside to cool in a non-metallic dish.

Rub the cooked ribs with the five-spice powder. Then combine all the remaining ingredients in a mixing bowl, season with salt and pepper, and pour over the ribs. Cover and leave to marinate in the refrigerator for at least 2 hours, but preferably overnight.

When you are ready to cook the ribs, preheat the oven to 190°C (375°F/Gas 5). Bring the ribs to room temperature then place them on a rack in a baking tray, reserving the marinade. Roast on the middle shelf of the oven for 20 minutes.

Brush the ribs with the marinade, turn them and then return to the oven and continue to roast for a further 20 minutes. Serve with steamed green vegetables or a side of Cook-up Rice (see page 167).

900 g (2 lb) pork ribs
2 teaspoons five-spice powder
2 garlic cloves, crushed
225 ml (8 fl oz/1 cup) dark soy sauce
2 tablespoons hoisin sauce
3 tablespoons rice wine
3 chunks fermented bean
    curd, crushed
4 tablespoons runny honey
salt and freshly ground
    black pepper

Chicken and Brandy Broth

This gentle and soothing recipe brings back happy memories of being looked after by my mum when I was feeling under the weather. She would always make this for us when we were poorly or needed cheering up. This soup, served with a kind, loving word, can make the world seem like a much better place.

SERVES *4*

50 g (2 oz/2 cups) dried
    Chinese mushrooms
20 g dried shrimps
1 tablespoon vegetable oil
1 large shallot, finely sliced
2 skinless chicken breast fillets,
    chopped into bite-sized pieces
1 birdseye chilli, halved, seeded
    and finely sliced
2 teaspoons caster (superfine) sugar
1 tablespoon light soy sauce
120 ml (4 fl oz/½ cup) brandy
6 slices of fresh ginger
500 ml (17 fl oz/2 cups)
    chicken stock
handful of spring onions
    (scallions), chopped
250 g (9 oz) vermicelli noodles
salt and freshly ground
    black pepper

Put the mushrooms and shrimps in a bowl. Cover with hot water and leave to soak for 20 minutes.

Meanwhile, heat the oil in a deep saucepan over a medium heat. Add the shallot and cook for about 4 minutes until soft. Then add the chicken pieces and sauté for about 5 minutes or until cooked through.

Stir in the chilli and sugar and cook until the sugar has dissolved. Add the soy sauce and season with salt and pepper. Pour in the brandy, stir in the ginger slices and simmer for 5 minutes. Drain the mushrooms and dried shrimps, reserving the soaking liquor. Chop the mushrooms and add to the saucepan together with the shrimps and liquor.

Pour in the chicken stock and continue to simmer for about 10 minutes or until the chicken is tender and the broth has reduced.

Before serving, add the spring onions and the vermicelli noodles and simmer for 3–5 minutes until the noodles are soft. Serve in warmed bowls.

Sweet 'n' Sour Chilli Beef Balls

SERVES 4–6

For the meatballs

500 g (1 lb 2 oz) minced
    (ground) beef

½ onion, grated

2 teaspoons garlic powder

1 tablespoon finely sliced spring
    onions (scallions)

1 tablespoon dark soy sauce

1 teaspoon Worcestershire sauce

½ teaspoon West Indian
    pepper sauce

1 egg, beaten

2 tablespoons fine breadcrumbs

1–2 tablespoons groundnut oil

salt and freshly ground
    black pepper

For the sweet and sour sauce

6 tablespoons white vinegar

6 tablespoons light brown sugar

4 tablespoons tomato ketchup

2 tablespoons dark soy sauce

2 tablespoons light soy sauce

1 tablespoon grated fresh ginger

1 tablespoon crushed garlic

2 bell peppers (red and yellow),
    roughly cubed

2 red chillies, halved, seeded
    and finely sliced

2 spring onions (scallions), finely
    sliced, garnish

To make the meatballs, put the mince in a mixing bowl. Add all the remaining ingredients and mix well with your hands. Roll the mixture into balls and set aside.

When you are ready to cook, heat the oil in large, deep frying pan over a medium heat. Add the meatballs and cook them for 5–10 minutes until they are browned on all sides.

For the sweet and sour sauce, pour the vinegar into a saucepan and heat gently. Add the sugar and stir until it has dissolved. Then stir in the tomato ketchup, soy sauces, ginger and garlic. Add the peppers and simmer gently for 5 minutes until they begin to soften. Increase the heat and stir until the sauce thickens.

Add the meatballs to the sweet and sour sauce and simmer for 5 minutes. Serve on warmed plates with egg or rice noodles and garnish with the spring onion.

Pork and Chicken Chow Mein

Chow mein is one of those dishes that doesn't really have a set recipe. It's a great way of using up leftovers and is equally good made with just vegetables. This version is my favourite combination. In the West Indies, chow mein is served as an accompaniment, but it is also a satisfying main course.

SERVES 4

Bring a deep saucepan of salted water to the boil. Add the noodles, reduce the heat and simmer as instructed on the pack until theyare cooked and soft. Drain the noodles, rinse under cold water and set aside.

Heat one tablespoon of the oil in a deep frying pan or wok over a medium heat. Add the eggs and cook them until they have scrambled. Scoop out of the pan and set aside.

Heat the remaining oil and add the chillies and vegetables. Stir-fry for about 5 minutes until they are just cooked and then add the pork and chicken. Stir in the noodles, combine well and fold in the scrambled eggs. Season with the soy sauce, salt, pepper and pepper sauce.

A few minutes before serving, stir in the bean sprouts and toss until they are warmed through but still crunchy. Then garnish with the sesame oil before serving in warmed bowls.

500 g (1 lb 2 oz) fresh egg noodles

2 tablespoons groundnut oil

3 eggs, lightly beaten

2 birdseye chillies, halved, seeded and finely sliced

1 small carrot, diced

50 g (2 oz/½ cup) green beans, sliced into 1 cm (½ in) lengths

50 g (2 oz/generous ⅓ cup) frozen peas

handful of spring onions (scallions), finely sliced

140 g (5 oz) Chinese barbecue pork, sliced

100 g (3½ oz) cooked chicken, shredded

2–3 tablespoons light soy sauce

½ teaspoon West Indian pepper sauce

2 handfuls of bean sprouts

few dashes of sesame oil, to garnish

salt and freshly ground black pepper

Rosemary was another of the great Georgetown beauties.
Her fair skin and mulato features were reminiscent of
the exotic screen goddesses of the day. Names such as
Ava Gardner, Merle Oberon and Claire Bloom were often
mentioned when Rosemary walked into a room.

Mum and Rosemary were neighbours, school friends
and close confidantes. The two girls were often mistaken
for sisters due to their physical resemblance
and their self-contained closeness was often excluding.
Each Sunday when the sun began to fall, Mum and
Rosemary, like a pair of naughty peacocks, would dress
up to the nines in their homespun Sunday best and waltz
past the liming 'sweet boys', giggling with linked arms.
all the way from Camp Street and up Lamaha Street
before turning on to Main Street. They loved the romance
of meandering under the shade of the flamboyant trees
while making their way to their final destination, the
seawall.

Just like on any other Sunday, the ritual was only
completed once the pretty teenagers paraded themselves
in front of the whole of Georgetown's society, from a turn
around the bandstand and up and down the promenade.
They laughed, joked and basked in the refracted warmth
of the impending twilight moon. The girls stared out on to
the horizon and over the ardent Atlantic Ocean, longing
for its undertow to throw them to lands far beyond their
imagination's reach. They yearned for adventures, yet
were shy of the unknown, and reticent to loosen the ties
that bound their sheltered, happy, young lives.

Late one night, Rosemary, along with most of the
inhabitants of Camp Street, was awakened by the
haunting sound of her mother howling in anguish.
Rosemary's beloved father had been robbed and left for
dead. The maturity that the girls craved was foisted upon
Rosemary cruelly and mercilessly. In one violent act,
Rosemary said goodbye to her childhood, her faith and her
innocence. It was decided that Rosemary should be sent
to boarding school in England, to recover from the family
tragedy and to better her prospects. The childhood friends

They yearned for
adventures, yet were
shy of the unknown,
and reticent to
loosen the ties
that bound their
sheltered, happy
young lives.

A Mulato's Prayer

Make me a bridge. O Lord my god
Between the different races.
Help me to reach the hearts and minds
Or those with different faces.

WATER STREET LOOKING SOUTH, GEORGETOWN, DEMERARA, BRITISH GUIANA

From the first day that I knew myself,
I never could quite see
Why God had made me different,
With no real identity.
Though other friends were like me
There was no one quite the same;
We were the rainbow children,
And they called us many names...

hugged a tearful farewell and said goodbye for ever as Rosemary boarded a steamship bound for Portsmouth.

One evening in 1988, Mum answered the telephone to a very English sounding lady. Distracted and busy, Mum didn't have any idea who she was speaking with and was about to slam the phone down when the voice said, 'Mausey, it's me!' Mum sat down on the floor and cried, 'Rosemary is that really you girl?' It had been 38 years since the friends had spoken to one another. Rosemary was taking evening classes in cake decoration and one night while mastering the art of sugar roses, one of her fellow students Yasmeen asked her where she was from. She asked because she thought Rosemary resembled her best friend's mother from Guyana.

Rosemary shrieked, 'Is her name Maureen?' The students put two and two together and my sister's best friend gave Rosemary our telephone number. The two women picked up where they had left off and didn't lose touch ever again. The tides of life had brought them back together. Rosemary and her husband Peter retired to Barbados and Mum and I visited them several times. With the help of her housekeeper Ophelia, Rosemary became an accomplished Caribbean cook and, to this day, entertains lavishly and with open arms. Looking every inch a film star, Rosemary stands at her stove for hours on end, wearing elaborate kaftans and dripping with gold jewellery frying Flying Fish for her friends in memory of her past life. She knew how much my Mum loved her Fried Fish (see page 139) and would always give her 100 pieces of the deliciously spicy fish (which had been frozen), to take back home with her to London to share among her family and their mutual friends. A silent gesture in appreciation of an enduring friendship.

Typical Demerara Hou

British Guiana

4 Seafood Specials

My a...
... ol...
wou...
the...
I c...
don...

sisters on the far side visiting

you occasionally. I am sure there
         be
would, a whole lot you were
miss away from Home — frien-
d above all your Home ties include
the love of a great Mother. She
never tires speaking of you to th
kind folks here & how well she
thinks you will get on with th
people you may meet. I am of
that opinion also, but you shoul
correct your moody disposition

Fried Fish with Salad

Rosemary's recipe should be shared with old friends and with a glass of June's Rum Punch (see page 232). The tasty, spicy breaded fillets are also delicious cold in a sandwich with a sprinkling of pepper sauce.

SERVES 4

Lay the fish flat in a dish, pour over the lime juice and season with salt and pepper. Add the pepper and Worcestershire sauces, then sprinkle over the paprika, garlic powder and parsley and rub all over the fish with your hands. Cover and leave to stand for 10 minutes.

Spread the flour on a flat plate and season with the mustard and garlic powder, dried thyme and cayenne pepper. On a second plate, spread out the breadcrumbs and in a bowl, beat the eggs.

Heat the oil and butter in a large frying pan over a medium heat. Take each piece of fish and dredge it in the plain flour, then the egg wash and then coat in the breadcrumbs. Carefully place into the oil and butter and fry for about 2 minutes on each side, or until golden brown. Lift out of the oil with a slotted spoon and drain on kitchen paper. Serve on warmed plates with a mixed salad and lemon wedges.

8 white fish fillets, such as flying
    fish, tilapia, sole or cod

juice of 1 lime

1 teaspoon West Indian
    pepper sauce

2 dashes of Worcestershire sauce

1 teaspoon sweet paprika

2 teaspoons garlic powder

2 teaspoons chopped parsley

150 g (5 oz/1 ³/₄ cup) plain
    (all-purpose) flour

2 teaspoons mustard powder

1 teaspoon garlic powder

½ teaspoon dried thyme

½ teaspoon cayenne pepper

150 g (5 oz/1³/₄ cups)
    fresh breadcrumbs

2 eggs

2 tablespoons groundnut oil, for frying

30 g (1 oz) salted butter

freshly ground black pepper

Red Snapper with Tomato Sauce

A Caribbean classic, this dish is delicious served with a helping of Cou-Cou (see page 118) or fresh, steamed rice.

SERVES 4

2 tablespoons mild olive oil

1 large onion, cut into rings

2 teaspoons soft brown sugar

2 garlic cloves, finely chopped

2 tablespoons tomato purée

200 ml (7 fl oz/generous ¾ cup)
  dry white wine

1 teaspoon dried oregano

1 teaspoon dried thyme

1 teaspoon paprika

½ teaspoon ground allspice

400 g (14 oz) tin can of
  chopped tomatoes

1 Scotch bonnet chilli, halved,
  seeded and finely sliced

1 teaspoon light soy sauce

1 teaspoon Worcestershire sauce

1 teaspoon West Indian
  pepper sauce

4 red snapper fillets, skin on,
  pin boned

juice of ½ lime

2 tablespoons finely chopped
  parsley, to garnish

For the red snapper, heat the oil in a lidded, large, heavy frying pan over a medium heat. Add the onion and cook for about 5 minutes until soft and translucent. Sprinkle over the sugar, then add the garlic and allow it to cook for a minute before adding the tomato purée. Stir well for a further minute.

Pour in the wine and allow the mixture to reduce a little. Next add the herbs and spices, tomatoes, chilli and the soy, Worcestershire and pepper sauces. Continue to cook the mixture on a gentle heat for about 5 minutes until the sauce has thickened.

Add the fish, flesh-side down, to the thickened tomato sauce. Cover and allow the fish to cook for about 5 minutes, turning once. Remove the lid from the fish and pour over the lime juice. Season with salt and pepper, if desired.

To serve, spoon some Cou-Cou (see page 118), or rice onto warmed plates, add the fish and top with the spicy tomato and onion gravy. Garnish with the parsley.

Shrimp Creole

This spicy recipe is as colourful and flavourful as the Caribbean itself.

SERVES 6

2 tablespoons mild olive oil

60 g (2 oz/¼ cup) salted butter

1 onion, halved and thinly sliced

3 garlic cloves, finely chopped

1 green pepper (bell pepper),
   halved, seeded and thinly sliced

1 Scotch bonnet chilli, halved,
   seeded and thinly sliced

2 celery sticks, finely sliced

60 g (2 oz/¼ cup) creamed
   coconut, cubed

1 tablespoon smoked paprika

2 teaspoons garlic powder

2 teaspoons soy sauce

2 teaspoons Worcestershire sauce

2 teaspoons West Indian
   pepper sauce

1 tablespoon tomato purée

large pinch of sugar

400 g (14 oz) tin can of
   chopped tomatoes

900 g (2 lb) tiger prawns (shrimp),
   peeled and deveined

salt and freshly ground
   black pepper

finely chopped parsley, to garnish

lemon wedges, to garnish

Heat the oil and butter in a saucepan or deep frying pan over a medium heat. When the butter has melted, add the onion, garlic, green pepper, chilli and celery and cook for about 5 minutes until softened. Add the creamed coconut and stir until melted.

Sprinkle over the paprika and garlic powder. Then add the soy, Worcestershire and pepper sauces, tomato purée and the sugar. Stir and cook for 5 minutes. Pour in the chopped tomatoes and simmer until the sauce has reduced by half. Finally, add the prawns and simmer for about 5 minutes or until they are cooked through.

Serve on warmed plates with Vegetable Yellow Rice (see page 160), garnished with finely chopped parsley and a lemon wedge.

Salt Fish and Green Bananas

This is one of St Lucia's national dishes. This is not a pretty dish, but it is highly nutritious and very tasty. The style of cooking has African origins and is typical of what locals eat in order to sustain themselves whilst working the land.

SERVES **6**

To cook the green bananas, put them in a saucepan and cover with water. Add 1 tablespoon of the oil and a half a teaspoon of salt. Bring the water to the boil and cook the bananas for a few minutes until the green skin of the bananas turn dark and begin to split. Drain and set aside to cool.

For the salt fish, heat the vegetable oil in a frying pan over a medium heat. Add the onions and garlic and cook for 2 minutes. Add the tomatoes together with a dash of water and cook for about 5 minutes until they soften and break down – this will create the delicious sauce.

Add the carrots and peppers to the pan and stir well. Cook for about 5 minutes until they become tender. Flake in the salt fish and stir well, then add the spring onions, turmeric, thyme and 500 ml (17 fl oz/2 cups) of water. Allow the mixture to cook until the vegetables are tender and the sauce has thickened.

Meanwhile, peel the bananas and cut them in half, then cut each half in two lengthways. Heat the remaining oil with the butter in a frying pan and, when bubbling, add the sugar and allow it to melt a little. Then place the bananas in the pan, flat-side down. Wait for them to brown and flip them over and allow the other side to brown too.

To serve, divide the fish and its sauce among warmed plates, top with the bananas and sprinkle with the chopped parsley.

For the green bananas

8–10 green bananas

2 tablespoons vegetable oil

2 tablespoons salted butter

3 tablespoons demerara sugar

salt and freshly ground
    black pepper

For the salt fish

2 tablespoons vegetable oil

2 onions, thinly sliced

4 garlic cloves, roughly chopped

6 tomatoes, chopped

2 carrots, thinly sliced at an angle

5 small coloured peppers
    (bell pepper),
    halved, seeded and diced

1½ lb (650 g) skinless salt cod fillet,
    prepared as on page 41

4 spring onions (scallions), chopped

2 heaped teaspoons turmeric

4 sprigs of fresh thyme

2 teaspoons West Indian
    pepper sauce

115 g (3½ oz/1½ cups) diced
    white cabbage

finely chopped parsley, to garnish

Tobagan Crab-Stuffed Avocado

This is perfect dinner party starter. The crab can be prepared well in advance and can be stuffed into the avocado at the last minute.

SERVES 4

450 g (1 lb) crab meat

juice of 1 lime

½ red onion, finely chopped

80 g (3 oz/½ cup) seeded and finely
  chopped watermelon

80 g (3 oz/½ cup) skinned, seeded
  and finely chopped cucumber

1 garlic clove, crushed

½ small yellow, red and green
  peppers(bell pepper) halved,
  seeded and finely sliced

1 tomato, diced

2 tablespoons finely
  chopped parsley

1 tablespoon finely chopped mint

2 large avocados, cut in half and
  stones removed

salt and freshly ground
  black pepper

flat leaf parsley, to garnish

For the green seasoning vinaigrette

2 teaspoons green seasoning

2 teaspoons dark rum

½ teaspoon soft brown sugar

100 ml (3½ fl oz/scant ½ cup) olive oil

Put the crab in a mixing bowl and pour over half of the lime juice. Add the red onion, watermelon, cucumber, garlic, scotch bonnets and tomato. Add salt and pepper and stir well.

Next make the green seasoning vinaigrette by putting the green seasoning, rum, sugar and the remaining lime juice into a small bowl. Season with a little salt and pepper and then whisk the mixture while slowly adding the olive oil.

Add the chopped herbs to the crab mixture and dress the crab with a few tablespoons of vinaigrette. Mix well so that all the crab is coasted and moist.

Fill the centre of each avocado half with the crab mixture. Drizzle a little more vinaigrette over each one and garnish with a sprig of parsley. Serve with warm Bakes (see page 198).

Nutmeg Prawns with Oil Down

The prawns can be prepared well in advance and the oiled down is very easy to make. They compliment each other surprisingly well in look and taste.

SERVES 4

Mix the marinade ingredients together in a bowl, season and add the prawns, coating well. Cover and leave to marinate in the refrigerator until ready to cook.

For the oil down, peel and cube the vegetables and put them into a large saucwater and bring to the boil. Reduce the heat and simmer for about 20 minutes until the vegetables are tender. Drain and leave to cool.

Heat the oil and butter in a heavy saucepan over a medium heat. Add the onions and cook until they soften then add the garlic and cook further. Mix the cooked vegetables in to the oil, stirring gently. Season with the pepper sauce, turmeric, thyme and nutmeg and sprinkle a pinch of salt and pepper.

Pour in the coconut milk, stir gently again and bring to the boil. Reduce the heat, cover and simmer for about 20 minutes.

Meanwhile, heat a griddle pan to high and slide four prawns on to 8 pre-soaked wooden skewers. Place the prawn skewers on the griddle and cook for 2 minutes on each side, drizzling the remaining marinade over the prawns as they are cooking.

Remove the lid from the oil down, add the beans and fresh thyme. Stir well allowing the beans to heat through. Divide the oil down among warmed plates and top each plate with two prawn skewers.

For the prawns and marinade

3 tablespoons nutmeg syrup
3 teaspoons light soy sauce
3 garlic cloves, crushed
2 teaspoons finely grated fresh ginger
2 teaspoons West Indian pepper sauce
½ teaspoon mixed spice
½ nutmeg, finely grated
2 tablespoons vegetable oil
32 raw prawns, shelled and deveined

For the oil down

2 tablespoons vegetable oil
2 tablespoons salted butter
1 large onion, diced
2 garlic cloves, chopped
1.5 kg (3 lb 5 oz) root vegetables
1 teaspoon West Indian pepper sauce
2 teaspoons turmeric
1 teaspoon dried thyme
¼ nutmeg, finely grated
400 ml (13 fl oz/1⅔ cups) coconut milk
125 g (4 oz/1 cup) green beans, cut, blanched and cooled
2 sprigs of thyme, leaves removed
salt and freshly ground black pepper

Each meal was symbolic of moments important to my family's history and a testament to our loved ones. They were accompanied by stories from a place referred to as 'home'.

Pumpkin and Shrimp

This is one of only two dishes that my father ever made. He must have been missing mother's cooking at the time ...

SERVES 4-6

1–2 tablespoons groundnut oil

1 onion, finely chopped

2 garlic cloves, crushed

2 chillies, halved, seeded and
    finely sliced

1 teaspoon West Indian
    pepper sauce

2 teaspoons chopped, fresh thyme

450 g (1 lb/3 cups) diced pumpkin
    (squash), cut into 2.5 cm
    (1 in) cubes

1 teaspoon caster (superfine) sugar

2 dashes of Worcestershire sauce

2 dashes of dark soy sauce

225 g (8 oz) raw prawns, shelled
    and deveined

salt and freshly ground
    black pepper

Heat the oil in a saucepan over a medium heat. Add the onion, garlic and chillies and cook for about 4 minutes until soft. Stir in the pepper sauce and thyme and cook for another couple of minutes.

Add the cubes of pumpkin and stir to coat them well before sprinkling with the sugar. Add 100 ml (3½ fl oz/scant ½ cup) of water, then reduce the heat, cover and simmer for about 20 minutes until the pumpkin starts to break down. Season with salt and pepper and the Worcestershire and soy sauces and roughly mash the pumpkin until it is lumpy but not puréed.

Add the prawns, put the lid back on the pan, and cook for another 5 minutes until the prawns are cooked through. This sweet and vibrant dish is lovely served with a chicken or vegetarian curry and steamed rice.

Marinated Sear-Grilled Tuna

As a lean fish, tuna tends to dry out quickly on the grill. Marinating and applying oil to the fish will help prevent this. Serve this grilled tuna with a sauce or fruity salsa.

SERVES 4

4 tuna steaks

grated zest and juice of 1 lime

½ tablespoon light soy sauce

2 spring onions (scallions),
     finely sliced

2 garlic cloves, crushed

2 tablespoons light olive oil

½ teaspoon onion powder

½ teaspoon garlic powder

½ teaspoon dried thyme

½ teaspoon dried cumin

½ teaspoon sweet paprika

salt and freshly ground
     black pepper

finely chopped parsley, to garnish

lime wedges, to garnish

To marinate the tuna steaks, put the fish in a non-metallic bowl. Mix all the remaining ingredients together, seasoning well, and pour over the tuna steaks. Cover and leave to marinate in the refrigerator for at least 1 hour.

When you are ready to cook, heat a grill pan until it is smoking and then sear each piece of tuna for 1 minute on each side.

Serve on warmed plates with salsa and stir-fried vegetables.

In my twenties, just as my mother had before me, I began to cook to reminisce and to heal. Somehow, the ritual of cooking and serving became a profound expression of who I am. It also enabled me to have a deeper understanding of my rich culinary heritage.

Blackened Creole Fish

The seasoning used in this recipe works particularly well on meaty firm fish fillets, such as salmon, tuna, cod or red snapper. Open the windows when cooking the fish – it can get VERY smoky!

SERVES 4

Dry the fish fillets and sprinkle with the lime juice. Season generously with salt and pepper.

Combine all the dry ingredients in a bowl and then pour into a dish for dredging. Brush each fish fillet on both sides with a little oil or melted butter (this is optional – salmon and tuna are oily and hold the seasoning really well). Dip the fish into the seasoning mix and coat well on both sides.

Heat the oil and butter in a large, heavy saucepan over a medium heat. When the butter has melted add the fish and cook it for about 1 minute on each side until it is just cooked through. The seasoning will turn quite black and will create a lot of smoke, but don't worry – that is how it should be. Serve immediately with a side of steamed, white rice.

4 firm fish fillets or steaks, such as salmon, tuna, cod or red snapper
juice of 1 lime
1 tablespoon sweet paprika
1 teaspoon cayenne pepper
2 teaspoons garlic powder
1 teaspoon onion powder
1 teaspoon dried thyme
1 teaspoon dried oregano
½ teaspoon allspice
2 tablespoons mild olive oil
1 tablespoon salted butter
a little oil or melted butter for brushing (optional)
salt and freshly ground black pepper

When I went to my
school friends' homes.
I realised my home
life was much more
dramatic than theirs.

Salmon Tartare with Corn Fritters

This easy dish makes an impressive starter, and goes great with a spiced up, crème fraîche dipping sauce.

SERVES 4

For the corn fritters

1 large cob of corn, kernals removed

75 g (3 oz) plain (all-purpose) flour

2 teaspoons sweet paprika

1 teaspoon English
    mustard powder

1 large egg

1 tablespoon milk

2 knobs of butter, melted

2 tablespoons vegetable oil
    for frying

salt and freshly ground
    black pepper

For the salmon tartare

450 g (1 lb) salmon, finely cubed

grated zest and juice of 1 lime

1 tablespoon mild olive oil

5 cm (2 in) piece of fresh
    ginger, grated

3 spring onions (scallions), chopped

2 birdseye chillies, halved, seeded
    and finely sliced

1 teaspoon finely chopped coriander
    (cilantro) leaves

1 dash of sesame oil

salt and freshly ground
    black pepper

Put the corn kernels in a pan of boiling salted water and cook for 3 minutes. Drain and rinse under a cold tap. Put the flour, paprika and mustard powder in a bowl. Beat the egg and milk together and pour slowly into the flour whilst mixing with a fork. Add the corn and season.

Heat 1 tablespoon of vegetable oil in wide frying pan, add 1 knob of butter and melt. Drop one tablespoon of the batter per fritter and fry on a low heat until set on the top and brown around the edges, and then turn over until cooked. Drain the fritters on kitchen paper and keep warm.

To marinate the salmon, put it in a non-metallic bowl. Pour over the lime juice and season well. Then add the oil, lime zest, ginger, spring onions, chillies and coriander. Cover and leave to marinate in the refrigerator for at least 30 minutes.

Just before serving, add a couple of dashes of sesame oil to the salmon tartare and stir to mix. Serve the salmon tartare with lime wedges and corn fritters. Also tastes great laced with a spiced-up crème fraîche alongside.

5 On the Side

Vegetable Yellow Rice

SERVES 4-6

1 teaspoon saffron strands

2 teaspoons vegetable oil

1 red onion, chopped

1 red pepper (bell pepper),
    halved, seeded and diced

1 carrot, diced

1 teaspoon chicken or
    vegetable seasoning

225 g (8 oz/generous 1 cup) easy
    cook, long grain rice

400 ml (14 fl oz/1²/₃ cups) vegetable
    or chicken stock

125 g (4 oz/1 cup) green
    beans, chopped

125 g (4 oz/1 cup) frozen peas

knob of butter

salt and freshly ground
    black pepper

Dissolve the saffron strands in 60 ml (2 fl oz/¼ cup) of boiling water and set aside.

Heat the oil in a saucepan over a medium heat. Add the onion and red pepper and cook for about 5 minutes until soft. Then add the carrot and season with salt and pepper and the chicken seasoning. Stir in the rice, mix well and pour in the saffron water, making sure that all the ingredients get a thorough coating.

Pour in the stock, stir and bring to the boil. Reduce the heat, cover and simmer for about 20 minutes. Then add the green beans and peas and cook for a further 5–10 minutes until the vegetables are tender and rice cooked through. Fluff the finished rice with a knob of butter and serve.

Vegetable Pelau

Simple, flavourful and nutritious, this is a great dish served on its own if you are dieting or recovering.

SERVES *6*

1 tablespoon vegetable oil

1 tablespoon brown sugar

340 g (12 oz/1²/₃ cups) brown rice, washed and drained

1 large onion, finely diced

2 garlic cloves, crushed

2 carrots, diced

100 g (2 oz) cauliflower

1 red pepper (bell pepper), halved, seeded and diced

3 celery sticks, sliced

2 large tomatoes, skinned, seeded and diced

handful of chopped spring onions (scallions)

2 tablespoons desiccated coconut

1 teaspoon dried thyme

West Indian pepper sauce, to taste

400 ml (13 fl oz/1²/₃ cups) coconut milk

150 ml (5 fl oz/²/₃ cup) vegetable or chicken stock

200 g (7 oz) green pigeon peas

salt and freshly ground black pepper

finely chopped parsley or coriander (cilantro) leaves, to garnish

Heat the oil in a large saucepan over a low heat, then add the sugar and let it melt and turn dark brown and bubbling, swirling the pan to even out the colouring if necessary. Stir in the rice to coat it thoroughly.

Add all the vegetables, grated coconut and thyme and season with salt pepper and pepper sauce to taste. Pour over the coconut milk and stock and bring the pan to the boil. Reduce the heat, cover and simmer or 25–30 minutes until the rice is tender.

Stir in the peas and cook for a further few minutes. Take the pan off the heat and leave the rice in the saucepan with the lid on for 5 minutes. Serve garnished with the parsley or coriander.

Creole Fried Rice

The six races that make up the Caribbean culinary melting pot have inspired this recipe. It's economical, nutritious and tasty.

SERVES 4

Heat 1 tablespoon of the groundnut oil in a wok over a medium-high heat until it is smoking. Reduce the heat then pour in the eggs and scramble until firm. Remove the eggs from the wok and set aside.

Heat the remaining oil and stir-fry the onion, garlic and ginger for about 4 minutes until the onion has softened. Increase the heat, then add the chicken and fry for another 4–5 minutes until cooked through and beginning to brown. Add the squash and cook for 2 minutes, then stir in soy and sweet chilli sauces. Combine the cold rice with the other ingredients in the wok and stir to heat through.

Stir in the salt fish and taste to check for seasoning (you may not need to add any salt). Return the scrambled eggs and mix. Serve the rice on a bed of shredded iceberg lettuce, garnished with chopped spring onions and a drizzle of the Indonesian sweet soy sauce.

2 tablespoons groundnut oil

3 eggs, beaten

1 onion, diced

2 garlic cloves, finely chopped

1 teaspoon finely grated
   fresh ginger

225 g (8 oz) minced
   (ground) chicken

80 g (3 oz) diced christophine
   (chayote) squash

1 tablespoon light soy sauce

2 teaspoons sweet chilli sauce

550 g (4 oz/3 cups) cold cooked
   white jasmine rice

80 g (3 oz) cooked salt cod, shredded

salt and freshly ground
   black pepper

iceberg lettuce, shredded, to serve

handful of sliced spring onions
   (scallions), to serve

Indonesian sweet soy sauce,
   to serve

often think of you & what life here would mean to you should you g[et] the opportunity. Though I hate it I c[...] [...] settling do[...] [...] brother & sis[...] [...] visiting you [...] sure th[...] wo[...] [...] mor[...] mi[...] [...] — frien[...] [...] above all Your Home ties include the Love of a great Mother. She never tires speaking of you to the Kind folks here & how well she thinks you will get on with the people you may meet. I am of that opinion also, but you shoul[d] correct your moody dispositio[n]

Cook-up Rice

Rice is eaten at least once a day in most West Indian households. Even if my mother made an alternative accompaniment for a meal, she always made sure that she had a rice dish on standby. In Guayana, where this dish originates, Cook-up Rice is a must have at meal times. This recipe can be made in a variety of ways and is a useful way of using up leftovers.

SERVES 4-6

Heat the oil in a deep heavy, saucepan over a medium heat. Add the onion, garlic and bacon and cook for about 5 minutes until the bacon is cooked through and the onion is translucent.

Sprinkle in the chilli or pepper sauce and stir in the creamed coconut until it has melted. Add the okras and peas, stir and season well with the thyme and salt and pepper.

Stir in the rice and mix well until all the ingredients are evenly distributed. Then increase the heat, pour in the chicken stock and bring it to the boil. Reduce the heat, give the contents of the pan a good stir, then cover and simmer for 15–20 minutes until the rice is tender and the liquid is absorbed.

Serve in warmed bowls and eat on its own or as an accompaniment to another meal.

1 tablespoon groundnut oil

1 onion, diced

2 garlic cloves, crushed

150 g (5 oz) bacon or pancetta, finely chopped

2 birdseye chillies, halved, seeded and finely sliced or

2 teaspoons West Indian pepper sauce

100 g (3½ oz/⅓ cup) creamed coconut, cubed

8 okra, sliced

425 g (15 oz) can of cooked black-eyed peas

1 teaspoon dried thyme

340 g (12 oz/1½ cups) easy cook, long grain rice

500 ml (18 fl oz/2¼ cups) chicken stock

salt and freshly ground black pepper

Corn on the Cob

These mini, easy-to-make corn on the cobs are full of flavour and are a great accompaniment to any Caribbean meal.

SERVES 4-6

250 ml (8½ fl oz/1 cup) coconut milk

375 ml (12 fl oz/1½ cups)
   chicken stock

4 corn on the cob, husks removed
   and snapped in half

leaves from 2 sprigs of fresh thyme

2 birdseye chillies, halved,
   seeded and finely chopped

2 tablespoons salted butter

salt and freshly ground
   black pepper

Pour the coconut milk and chicken stock into a saucepan and heat to a gentle simmer. Add the corn and the remaining ingredients.

Cover and cook for 20–30 minutes until most of the liquid has absorbed and the corn is cooked. You should be left with a lovely glossy sauce that you can pour over the corn, to serve.

Sweetcorn Pudding

Comfort food at its best! This family favourite is wonderful served with baked ham, fried chicken, spare ribs or meatloaf – pretty much anything other than curry.

SERVES 4

250 ml (8½ fl oz/1 cup)
    evaporated milk

3 eggs

60 g (2 oz/¼ cup) butter, melted

175 g (6 oz/generous 1 cup)
    fine cornmeal

1 small onion, grated

400 g (14 oz) can of creamed
    style corn

200 g (7 oz/1 cup) fresh or
    tinned corn kernels

30 g (1 oz) diced red
    peppers (bell peppers)

30 g (1 oz) diced green peppers
    (bell peppers)

1 teaspoon West Indian
    pepper sauce

2 teaspoons English
    mustard powder

125 g (4 oz/1 firmly packed cup)
    strong cheddar, grated

salt and freshly ground
    black pepper

Preheat the oven to 190°C (375°F/Gas 5) and lightly grease a 1.5 litre (2½ pints/6¼ cups) baking dish with butter.

Pour the evaporated milk into the dish and beat in the eggs and melted butter. Add the cornmeal and beat well once more. Then stir in the onion, creamed corn, corn kernels and mixed peppers. Season well with salt and pepper and the pepper sauce and mustard powder. Cover with the grated cheese and bake for 45–55 minutes until the pudding is browned and firm to the touch.

Sweet Potato and Yam Gratin

Because of my sweet tooth, I adore the combination of sweet onions and yams with even sweeter potatoes.

SERVES 4-6

Preheat the oven to 180°C (350°F/Gas 4) and prepare a baking dish by greasing it lightly with butter.

Heat the butter (being careful not to burn it) in a frying pan and sauté the onion and garlic until soft and translucent.

Arrange a layer of sweet potato on the bottom of the baking dish and top with a layer of onions, a sprinkling of garlic and season with salt and pepper. Cover with a layer of yams and repeat this layering process until all the potatoes and yams are used up.

Combine the double cream with the milk, mustard powder, pepper sauce and herbs. Season with a little salt and pepper.

Pour the seasoned cream in to the baking dish over the sweet potatoes and yams and top with the grated cheese .

Bake in the centre of the oven for 1½ -2 hours until the potatoes are tender and the topping golden brown.

30 g (1 oz) salted butter

1 large white onion, thinly sliced into rings

3 garlic cloves, crushed

450 g (1 lb) sweet potato, peeled and thinly sliced

450 g (1 lb) yams, peeled and thinly sliced

350 ml (11 fl oz/1¹/₃ cups) double (thick) cream

2 teaspoons English mustard powder

1 teaspoon West Indian pepper sauce

125 g (4 oz) mature cheddar, grated

salt and freshly ground black pepper

Fried Okra with Tomatoes

Although a healthier version of a traditional Southern-style veggie, this recipe does not lack in flavour – the combination of okra with tomatoes, is simply delicious.

SERVES 4-6

Heat the oil in a deep, heavy frying pan over a medium heat. Add the onion and sauté for about 5 minutes until soft and translucent. Add all the remaining ingredients, combine well, cover and simmer for 15 minutes.

Check for seasoning and serve straight away.

1 tablespoon vegetable oil

1 onion, thinly sliced into rings

450 g (1 lb) okra, trimmed

3 garlic cloves, crushed

juice of ½ lemon

1 red pepper (bell pepper),
    halved, seeded and diced

2 green chillies, halved,
    seeded and finely sliced

400 g (14 oz) can of
    chopped tomatoes

½ teaspoon dried thyme

salt and freshly ground
    black pepper

Sautéd Bora

Bora beans, also known as yard long beans, are used in most West Indian cuisines. They are best stir-fried with potatoes and shrimp, and can be finely chopped into chow mein.

SERVES 4-6

2 tablespoons groundnut oil

1 onion, halved and finely sliced

2 garlic cloves, crushed

2 teaspoons grated fresh ginger

1 Scotch bonnet chilli, halved,
    seeded and finely sliced

½ teaspoon garam masala

1 teaspoon ground cumin

3 tomatoes, chopped

450 g (1 lb) bora beans, trimmed and
    sliced into 2.5 cm (1 in)
    wide strips

1 teaspoon West Indian
    pepper sauce

salt and freshly ground
    black pepper

Heat the oil in a deep frying pan over a medium heat. Add the onion and garlic and sauté for about 5 minutes until soft. Add the ginger, chilli, garam masala and cumin and cook for a further 2 minutes.

Stir in the tomatoes and bora beans, then pour in 60 ml (2 fl oz/¼ cup) of water. Season well with salt and pepper and the pepper sauce and bring to the boil. Reduce the heat, cover and simmer for 8–10 minutes until the bora beans are tender.

'Buss up Shirt'

This Trinidadian paratha roti has its name because it resembles a burst open shirt. I adore rotis of any description, but this one is my absolute favourite.

MAKES 6

Sieve together the flour, baking soda and salt into a mixing bowl. Gradually add 450 ml (15 fl oz/1³/4 cups) warm water and, using your fingers, mix into a soft dough. There is no need to knead the dough, just bring it together in a soft, slightly sticky ball. Cover with the vegetable oil, then cover the bowl with clingfilm and rest for 20 minutes.

Combine the ghee and groundnut oil into a paste and set aside.

Turn out the dough on to a floured work surface and cut it into 6 equal pieces. With floured hands, form balls out of each piece and roll them out until they are as thin as possible.

For each roti, cut a line half way down the middle and brush the roti with a layer of the ghee and oil paste. Roll the dough into a cone shape, fold the open ends of the cylinder back into itself, pinch closed and roll into a ball. Repeat for each roti.

Roll out the balls again and, cooking individually, place each roti on an oiled and hot flat heavy pan. Turn over once browned and brush with oil. Continue to flip until cooked, around 3 or so minutes. Beat with a wooden spoon until flaky and slightly shredded and serve immediately.

450 g (1 lb/3½ cups) plain
   (all-purpose) flour
1 tablespoon baking powder (soda)
½ teaspoon salt
1 teaspoon vegetable oil
2 tablespoons ghee or butter
1 tablespoon groundnut oil

Callaloo and Crab

Though callaloo leaves give the most authentic West Indian flavour to this dish, you can use chard, kale or spinach instead.

SERVES 6

1 tablespoon vegetable oil

1 onion, chopped

3 garlic cloves, crushed

1 Scotch bonnet chilli, halved,
    seeded and finely sliced

450 g (1 lb/10 cups) chopped
    callaloo or spinach

450 g (1 lb) okra, sliced

600 ml (20 fl oz/2½ cups)
    coconut milk

1 tablespoon salted butter

500 g (1 lb 2 oz) cooked
    white crab meat

salt and freshly ground
    black pepper

Heat the oil in a large saucepan over a medium heat. Add the onion and fry for about 5 minutes until it is soft, then add the garlic and chilli and fry for a few more minutes.

Add the callaloo or spinach, a handful at time, and cover until it is wilted, which will be a matter of moments. Add the okra, pour over the coconut milk and stir in the butter. Re-cover the pan, reduce the heat and simmer for about 20 minutes. Add the crab meat and simmer for a further 10 minutes. Season well with salt and pepper and serve.

The Chinese adore chubby babies of which
I was a great specimen. The Caribbeans
love feeding people and, as I grew up, my
Caribbean aunts gauged the level of my
affections for them by how much of their
food I ate; so unsurprisingly, I became
obsessed with food at an early age.

Roti

MAKES *8* ROTI

225 g (8 oz/1¾ cups) plain
    (all-purpose) flour
1 tablespoon baking powder (soda)
1 teaspoon vegetable oil, plus extra
    for cooking
60 g (2 oz/¼ cup) salted butter

Sieve the flour and baking powder into a mixing bowl. Gradually add 160 ml (6 fl oz/¾ cup) water and, using your fingers, mix into a soft dough. There is no need to knead the dough, just bring it together in a soft ball. Cover with the 1 teaspoon of vegetable oil, then cover the bowl with clingfilm and rest for 30 minutes.

Roll the dough into a sausage and cut into eight equal pieces, then roll out each piece thinly into flat circles.

Heat an oiled frying pan over a medium heat. Add the roti, one by one, and cook for about 30 seconds, turning a couple of times and brushing with oil to prevent them from sticking.

Remove from the heat and clap between your hands to remove the air and to make the roti lovely and flaky.

Dhal Puri Roti

To make the rotis, sieve the flour and baking powder into a mixing bowl and add the salt. Gradually add 300 ml (10 fl oz/1¼ cups) of warm water and, using your fingers, mix into a soft dough. There is no need to knead the dough, just bring it together in a soft, slightly sticky ball. Cover with the vegetable oil, then cover the bowl with clingfilm and rest for 30 minutes.

For the dhal filling, put the split peas into a saucepan, cover with water and bring to the boil. Reduce the heat and simmer for 15–20 minutes until just tender. Transfer the split peas into a food processor and pulse until they resemble coarse breadcrumbs.

Add the remaining ingredients to the food processor and season well with salt and pepper. Pulse again until they are finely ground.

Cut the dough into 8 equal pieces and roll them into balls. Flatten each ball in the palm of your hands and add 1–2 tablespoons of the dhal mixture to the centre of each circle. Gather the edges around the filling and pinch tightly to seal. Gently roll into a ball once again and then, on a floured surface, roll out the dough to about 20–25 cm (8–10 in) diameter.

Heat an oiled frying pan over a medium heat. Add the roti, one by one, and cook for about 30 seconds or until golden, turning a couple of times and brushing with oil to prevent them from sticking. Repeat for each roti.

For the roti

450 g (1 lb/3½ cups) plain (all- purpose) flour

2 teaspoons baking powder (soda)

large pinch of salt

120 ml (4 fl oz/½ cup) vegetable oil, plus extra for frying

For the dhal filling

225 g (8 oz/1 cup) yellow split peas

4 garlic cloves, crushed

1 teaspoon ground turmeric

2 teaspoons ground cumin

1 teaspoon West Indian pepper sauce

salt and freshly ground black pepper

Caramelised Fried Plantain

SERVES 4

2 large ripe plantain
(dark skinned)
1 tablespoon vegetable oil
2 tablespoons salted butter
1 tablespoon demerara sugar
pinch of salt

Peel the plantain and cut on an angle into 5 mm (¼ in) thick slices.

Heat the oil in heavy-based frying pan over a medium heat, then add the butter and melt until foaming.

Fry the plantain on both sides for about 2–3 minutes until they are light brown. Sprinkle over the sugar and salt and continue to cook on both sides until the sugar is caramelised. Serve immediately.

BAO's

These lovely, little, steamed buns are particularly popular in Guyana, Trinidad and Jamaica where there is a Chinese heritage. My simple dough recipe is yeast free, very spongy and won't look as white and bready as they do in most dim sum restaurants. The filling suggestions included with the dough are a few of my favourites. You don't have to make them all – each set of ingredients fills 6 buns

MAKES **6** BUNS

For the dough

175 g (6 oz/1½ cups) plain
  (all-purpose) flour
2 teaspoons baking powder (soda)
20 g (¾ oz) lard or butter
50 g (2 oz/scant ¼ cup) caster
  (superfine) sugar
100 ml (3½ fl oz/scant ½ cup)
  warm milk
baking parchment cut into 7.5 cm
  (3 in) squares

For a char sui in barbecue sauce filling

1-½ teaspoon cornflour
  (cornstarch)
175 g (6 oz) char sui, diced
1 tablespoon soy sauce
1 tablespoon hoisin sauce
1 tablespoon caster
  (superfine) sugar
1 teaspoon sesame oil

To make the dough, sift the flour and baking powder into a bowl and rub in the lard. Add the sugar, pour in the warm milk and mix into a soft dough.

With well-floured hands (the dough is soft and sticky) remove the dough from the bowl and roll it into a sausage. Divide the dough into six equal pieces. Roll into balls in the palm of your hand and then flatten into discs.

Place a teaspoon of your chosen filling (ingredients list) in the centre of each disc and gather up the edges around the filling, sealing tightly. Place the bun, sealed-side down, on a square of baking parchment and steam over simmering boiling water for about 25 minutes until the filling is cooked through and the dough is slightly puffed and translucent.

To make the char sui in barbecue sauce filling, mix the cornflour with 100 ml (3½ fl oz/scant ½ cup) of water and pour into a saucepan. Add all the remaining ingredients and simmer gently until the sauce is thick and syrupy.

For a chicken and mushroom filling

For a chicken and mushroom filling

1 tablespoon vegetable oil

450 g (1 lb) minced (ground) chicken

1 carrot, finely chopped

1 tablespoon grated fresh ginger

3 garlic cloves, crushed

2 dried Chinese mushrooms, soaked,
    rinsed (but reserving the
    soaking liquid) and finely sliced

75 ml (21/2 fl oz/scant 1/3 cup)
    rice wine or sherry

175 g (6 oz/generous 1 cup) water
    chestnuts, minced

1 teaspoon soy sauce

2 tablespoons oyster sauce

3 tablespoons hoisin sauce

3 spring onions (scallions),
    finely chopped

salt and freshly ground
    black pepper

For a vegetarian filling

100 g (31/2 oz) kimchee

2 garlic cloves, crushed

6 dried Chinese mushrooms, soaked
    and finely chopped

large pinch of five-spice powder

1/2 teaspoon West Indian
    pepper sauce

2 spring onions (scallions),
    finely sliced

1 teaspoon sweet chilli sauce

1 teaspoon hoisin sauce

salt and freshly ground
    black pepper

To make the chicken and mushroom filling, heat the oil in a large frying pan over a medium heat. Add the chicken and fry for about 5 minutes until it is brown all over. Add the carrot, ginger and garlic and stir until well combined. Then stir in the mushrooms with some of the soaking liquor together with the rice wine and water chestnuts. Season with salt and pepper, add the three seasoning sauces and simmer until the stock has reduced by half before adding the spring onions.

For the vegetarian filling combine all the ingredients in a bowl.

Black Cake

Whenever I hear the word Christmas I think of three things: Pepperpot, Garlic Pork and Black cake, not the three wise men!

Most of my earliest memories are of Christmas time, decorating the tree and arguing with my siblings over whose turn it was to place the angel on the top of it. The wonderful smells of festive foods and the smiling faces of family and friends whose company I will eternally mourn.

One particular year, when I was about four or five, a large parcel arrived by special delivery from my maternal grandmother in Guyana. The box was covered in colourful stamps depicting exotic birds and flora and fauna indigenous to the Caribbean.

I was beside myself with anticipation and excitement, presuming that the box was full of gifts for me. My brother, sister and I followed our mother into the kitchen and watched avidly as she carefully opened the large box and revealed an ornate circular tin. The pretty antique tin was decorated in pastel shades of coral pink and mint green with a gold-filigreed trim around its circumference. As Mum removed the lid our eager eyes widened with anticipation, expecting to discover a plethora of treasures. However, our expectations were abruptly thwarted on discovering that the tin contained nothing more than a cake. An air

of disappointment loomed, visible on all faces apart from that of my mother's. Her expression lay somewhere between happiness, sadness and longing.

Oblivious to her surroundings, she removed the lid of the tin and gazed at the white cake that lay cushioned on top of discoloured wax paper, resplendent with royal icing adornments. She shut her eyes, held the tin to her face and inhaled. The aromas of her childhood memories flooded her heart and tears rolled down her cheeks. She felt the warmth of her mother's embrace and for a moment, she believed that she was home. I was deflated and felt let down by the grandparents I was yet to meet. As my interest waned, a heady scent unlike any I had ever experienced before struck me and I became intrigued.

As if by instinct my mother's eyes opened. She glared at us, slammed the tin shut and with a wagging finger exclaimed 'Do not even think of going anywhere near this tin until Christmas day. You'll be in big trouble if you do! And I mean it!'

Mum hid the tin and my brother and I were determined to find it. Later that very day, after a thorough search of the upstairs, my brother pushed me into the cupboard under the stairs. Through a smothering thicket of dark winter coats out popped my head, bang into a shelf. I looked up and spotted the tin, my arms raised to grab it 'It's here. I've found it!' I yelled.

My brother yanked me back through the woollen jungle and said 'Well, now we know where it is, we should do as we were told and leave it alone.' I was confused but I knew he was right. There was something about the tender sincerity in our mother's expression that touched our hearts, and, for the first time in our lives, we felt bound to honour her wishes.

Christmas Day meant 'open house' in Worton Way. Each year our modest home was bursting at the seams with relatives, friends and lost souls with nowhere else to go. Everyone who came shared what we had and never left hungry. My mother worked tirelessly to ensure that she could 'save face' and never be accused of under catering. When Christmas day finally arrived, I was given my first taste of what my mother described as 'the real black cake. Guyanese, the best in the Caribbean!'

I took a bite and was completely unimpressed – I didn't understand what all the fuss was about. The cake's deep black colour and soggy alcohol-soaked texture was completely foreign to me. Fragments of mixed fruits got stuck between my teeth, and the marzipan and royal icing stuck to the roof of my mouth.

Unhappily, I found solace through the familiarity, in a tin of Quality Street and ate several toffees in order to get rid of the taste of the black cake. Mum cut up her mother's cake into bite-sized pieces, and arranged them neatly on a silver tray that was etched with impressions of Guyana's most famous landmarks. Being the youngest (so technically the cutest) the tray was thrust into my hands and I was *instructed to smile and to go and serve the cake. I watched as our guests sank their teeth into the festive treat. The room hushed with contended sighs of pleasure. The flavours of the homeland that they had left behind filled them with contentment, nostalgia and sadness, and in some cases regret.*

However, before long the festivities resumed and raucous laughter could be heard from almost a block away. We danced the night away to Calypso's, The Sandpiper's and various reggae hits of the times. It was several years before I understood what the fuss was about and it is now my absolute favourite fruit cake.

Due to political unrest my maternal grandparents, Cyril and Maude, moved to the UK in early 1970s. Citizens of the new Co–operative Republic of Guyana were only allowed to leave their country with fifteen dollars in their pockets. As such they arrived in the UK on a cold winter's day like refugees, with few possessions and just thirty dollars. England too was suffering from political unrest, high inflation, miners strikes, the 'three-day week' and power shortages. Maude, however, was past caring about politics and was just thrilled to be reunited with her daughter and savored every second of her time spent with her grandchildren.

Mum and Granny spent many hours together in the kitchen, preparing and sharing each other's recipes. During these precious moments they did their best to make up for lost time, and they delighted in the discovery of the women that they had become.

As Christmas approached, during that winter of discontent, Granny decided that it was time to teach Mum how to make black cake. Much to her sadness, Granny had not been present at any of her children's weddings. She was denied the pleasure of baking black cakes for her two daughters' special days (a joyous Caribbean tradition). However, on their first attempt, this symbolic right of passage was rudely interrupted by a power cut, which struck right in the middle of baking. The cake was ruined and both women were more disappointed than I could have ever imagined.

Granny had died by the following winter, and I believe her last year with us in England to be one of the happiest in her short life. Mum spent the rest of her life trying to cook as well as her mother and perfecting her black cake recipe. Her proudest moments were watching her son and daughter cutting into the cakes that she had lovingly prepared for them on their wedding days. The following recipe is as close as I can get to my mother's, as she left no formal recipe for it – just a few scribbles on a old stained exercise book. However, the key to a truly successful black cake is trial and error mixed with a mother's love!

I love this picture of my mum and my
aunty Nipsey cooking up a storm in our
kitchen. Spending time with them as they
prepared the next delicious meal was one
of my favourite pastimes as a child.

6 Cakes and Bakes

Caribbean Black Cake

This deliciously rich and moist fruit cake is traditionally served at Christmas and weddings. Every Caribbean family has their own secret recipe for black cake, and this one is based on my grandmother Maude's. Over the years my mum then refined it further, and thankfully left the measurements below in an old stained exercise book. This cake never fails to impress.

MAKES *16-20* SERVINGS

340 g (12 oz/scant 2 cups) mixed fruit

114 g (4 oz/¼ cups) Maraschino glace cherries

2 teaspoon mixed Caribbean essence

1 teaspoon baking powder

30 ml (1 fl oz) dark rum

30 ml (1 fl oz) cherry brandy

4 tablespoons demerara sugar

114 g (4 oz) lightly salted butter

150 g (5 oz/³/₄ cup) granulated white sugar

3 eggs

114 g (4 oz/1 cup) self-raising flour

1 teaspoon mixed spice

1 teaspoon vanilla extract

1 teaspoon almond essence

Pre heat the oven to 170°c/325°f/Gas mark 3.

To prepare the fruit combine the mixed fruit and glace cherries. Take out a quarter of the fruit and set aside. Coarsely grind the remaining fruit and combine with the whole fruit. Place the fruit in an airtight jar and mix with 2 teaspoons of mixed Caribbean essence and 1 teaspoon of baking powder. Pour over 25ml (½ tablespoon) of dark rum and 25ml (½ tablespoon) of cherry brandy. Cover the jar securely and leave the fruit to steep in a cool dark place for at least two weeks.

To make the burnt sugar syrup place four tablespoons of brown Demerera sugar in deep saucepan and heat over a medium- high heat. Stir continuously with a wooden spoon until the sugar melts and starts to bubble. Turn the heat down to low and continue to stir until the sugar turns dark brown (almost black) Remove from the heat and slowly add two tablespoons of hot water and stir until the mixture is syrupy and resembles molasses. Allow to cool before use.

To make the cake batter place the butter in a mixing bowl and bring to room temperature. Add the sugar and beat until pale. Add the eggs, one at a time and mix well. Sift in slowly and fold in until smooth. Add the mixed spice, vanilla and almond essence. Drain the fruit, stir into in the cake batter and mix well.

Add enough burnt sugar syrup to make the batter dark brown.

Grease and line two 8 inch (20cm) spring form cake tins. Divide the cake mixture between the pans and bake on the middle shelf for one and half hours or until a cocktail stick comes out of the middle of the cake clean. When the cake is cooked, remove from the oven and let cool in the tin. Make several holes around the top of the cakes with a skewer and pour over the remaining 5 ml of rum and 5ml of cherry brandy.

Cover the cakes tins with foil and cling film and leave for 24 hours, for the alcohol to absorb and the flavours to develop.

Serve on it's own or add marzipan and royal icing if you are using it for a wedding, christening or Christmas cake.

Mummy's Portuguese Pancakes with Spiced Sugar Syrup

My mother always served this traditional delicacy on Shrove Tuesday and called them Portuguese pancakes. We loved them so much when we were kids, but we never thought to ask why we were served them instead of the usual, pan-fried British equivalent. As we only ate them once a year, Mum would make dozens of the delicious hollow eggy golden balls and send me out to her favourite neighbours with bowls full of the pancakes drenched in sticky clear syrup. She used three frying pans for this epic cook-in and it was always a day's work for Mum, so it's no wonder that she could only face cooking them once a year.

By the early nineties, my dad had died and we had all left home. Mum moved to a small flat with a heartbreakingly small kitchen, so I thought I would never eat Portuguese pancakes again. Then, one Christmas, I took Mum to Portugal for her birthday. We spent the first night in Lisbon and at breakfast the next morning, there on the Continental buffet table sat a huge bowl of Mum's pancakes next to a jug of clear syrup. We were jubilant and hoped we would have them for breakfast every day for the rest of our tour. Alas, we never found them again, anywhere.

SERVES *10*

For the pancakes
225 g (8 oz/scant 1 cup)
     unsalted butter
450 g (1 lb/3½ cups) plain
     (all-purpose) flour
2 teaspoons vanilla extract
12 eggs
groundnut or corn oil for frying
icing (confectioners') sugar,
     for dusting

For the sugar syrup
450 g (1 lb/2 cups) sugar
½ teaspoon ground mixed spice
1 cinnamon stick, broken in half

Pour 450 ml (15 fl oz/scant 2 cups) of water into a saucepan, add the butter and bring to the boil. Reduce the heat to low and beat in the flour, until the mixture leaves the sides of the pan. Stir in the vanilla extract. Take the saucepan off the heat and combine the eggs into the batter, one at a time.

Heat the oil in a deep-fat fryer until it's smoking. With a teaspoon, drop balls of the mixture into the hot oil and fry 2–3 minutes or until golden. Remove the balls from the oil with a slotted spoon and drain on kitchen paper.

To make the syrup, pour 300 ml (10 fl oz/1¼ cups) of water into a saucepan. Add the sugar and, over a medium heat, let it dissolve and then bring it to the boil. Add the mixed spice and cinnamon stick. Serve with a drizzle of syrup and a dusting of icing sugar.

Bakes

Serve these delicious breads with salt fish or Salt Fish and Ackee (see page 41), stuff with fried fish or simply serve as you would any bread accompaniment.

SERVES *6*

225 g (8 oz/1³/₄ cups) plain
    (all-purpose) flour
2 teaspooons baking powder (soda)
1/2 teaspooon ground cinnamon
1/2 teaspooon salt
30 g (1 oz) lard, chilled and diced
1 tablespoon caster
    (superfine) sugar
150 ml (5 fl oz/²/₃ cup) milk
vegetable oil, for deep frying

Sift the dry ingredients into a mixing bowl. Rub in the lard until the mixture resembles breadcrumbs.

Dissolve the sugar in the milk and pour over the dry mixture. Stir it until a soft dough is formed and then knead the dough for a minute on a floured surface. Cover and put in the refrigerator for 30 minutes.

Knead the rested dough for another minute, then pull off walnut-sized pieces. Roll each piece of dough in the palm of your hand into balls and flatten into 1 cm (½ in) thick, 10 cm (4 in) diameter circles.

Pour enough oil into a deep heavy saucepan to cover the puffed-up bakes. Heat on a medium heat until the oil is 176°C (350°F), then add the bakes, in batches if necessary, and fry for about 2–3 minutes until the bakes puff up and float to the surface. Use a slotted spoon to remove the bakes from the pan and drain on kitchen paper.

Aunty Thelma's Sponge Cake

Mum always had a homemade sponge and cheese straws at the ready in case anyone popped in. This sponge recipe was Mum's favourite, and comes from my Aunty Thelma, who was in fact my dad's cousin.

SERVES **4-6**

Preheat the oven to 180°C (375°F/Gas 4) and grease and line a 20 cm (8 in) cake tin.

Put the eggs, sugar and melted butter, together with 1 tablespoon of water, into a bowl. Using a handheld mixer, beat the mixture for about 20 minutes until it is thick and creamy.

Gradually fold in the flour and lemon zest, then pour the mixture into the prepared cake tin and bake on the middle shelf for 45–60 minutes, until a skewer pushed into the centre of the cake comes out cleanly.

5 large eggs
200 g (7 oz/scant 1 cup) caster (superfine) sugar
1 tablespoon melted unsalted butter
200 g (7 oz/1²/₃ cups) fine sponge flour, sifted
finely grated zest of ½ lemon

Tri-Colour Cake

I first made this cake when I was eight years old. Curry was cooking on the stove and Mum was making split pea soup in her new pressure cooker that scared us all. She seemed irritated that I looked so bored and said to me gruffly, 'Why don't you make a cake instead of just sitting there doing nothing?' For three decades I tried to convince her to change the name to marble cake, but she was having none of it .

SERVES *8-10*

225 g (8 oz/scant 1 cup) margarine
    or butter

400 g (14 oz/1²/₃ cups) caster
    (superfine) sugar

4 eggs

500 g (1 lb 2 oz/4 cups) plain
    (all-purpose) flour

4 teaspoons baking powder (soda)

300 ml (10 fl oz/1¹/₃ cups) milk

2 tablespoons cocoa powder
    or drinking chocolate

1 teaspoon almond essence

1 teaspoon yellow liquid
    food colouring

1 teaspoon vanilla extract

½ teaspoon red liquid
    food colouring

1 teaspoon Caribbean mixed
    essence or 1 tablespoon
    dark rum

For the chocolate icing

225 g (8 oz/scant 1 cup)
    unsalted butter

450 g (1 lb/3²/₃ cups) icing sugar

4 tablespoons cocoa powder

2 tablespoons milk

Preheat the oven to 190°C (375°F/Gas 5). Grease and flour a 20 cm (8 in) round cake tin.

In a large mixing bowl, cream the margarine and sugar until pale and light with a handheld electric mixer. Still beating, add the eggs 1 at a time and combine. Gradually sift in the flour and baking powder and mix through. Carefully stir in the milk. The batter is slightly thinner than most.

Divide the cake mixture into three separate bowls. In one bowl, add the cocoa powder and almond essence and mix well. In the second, add the yellow food colouring and vanilla extract and mix well. In the third, add enough red food colouring for the mixture to turn bright pink and the Caribbean mixed essence.

Place spoonfuls of the three batters into the prepared tin, alternating colours, then insert a skewer into the cake mix and make a few random, gentle swirls. Bake for about 1 hour until a skewer inserted in the centre of the cake comes out clean. Don't worry or be surprised if the top of the cake splits.

Let the cake cool slightly in its tin before turning onto a wire wrack and leaving it to reach room temperature. To make the icing, put all the ingredients into a bowl and mix to combine. Using a palette knife, smooth the icing all over the cake before cutting into slices to serve.

Tau Sar Cakes

Chinese Caribbeans are renowned for patisserie in the West Indies and loved in Guyana for black bean cakes, char sui baus, tennis rolls, pandan chiffon cakes and rich sponge cakes. My aunts Moi and May's recipe was legendary in Georgetown and they left behind them a generation of frustrated cooks whose Tau Sar will never taste as sweet as theirs. I hope that you'll love these delicious dainties as much as I do.

MAKES *8* CAKES

For the filling
450 g (1 lb/2¼ cups) dried
    black-eyed peas
an equal weight of muscovado
    sugar once the beans are cooked
    (see Steps 1 and 2)
600 ml (17 fl oz/2 cups) vegetable oil

For the pastry
200 g (7 oz/¹/₃ cup) lard or butter,
cut into cubes
375 g (13 oz/3 cups) plain
    (all-purpose) flour
red food colouring

For the filling, put the beans in a bowl, cover with water and soak overnight. Drain the beans, then place them in a saucepan, cover with fresh water and bring to the boil. Reduce the heat and simmer for 30 minutes until soft.

Drain the beans and blend into a paste in a food processor. Then sieve to remove any skins. Weigh the bean paste and add the same amount of muscovado sugar. Place both in a saucepan over a medium-high heat. Stir until the sugar dissolves and begins to thicken.

Add the oil and reduce the heat. Continue to cook for about 45 minutes, stirring constantly, until it thickens and comes away from the sides of the pan. Remove the pan from the heat and set aside.

To make the pastry, in a large mixing bowl, rub the lard or butter into 250 g (9 oz/2 cups) of the flour with your fingertips until the mixture resembles breadcrumbs. Take out a large handful, squeeze it together and set aside.

Add the remaining flour to the mixture left in the bowl and combine. Make a well in the centre and pour in 170 ml (6 fl oz/³/₄ cup) of cold water. Fold all the

ingredients together and form a ball with your
hands and then shape it into a roll. Pull off small
pieces and flatten them in the palms of your hands.

Place a small amount of the remaining breadcrumb
mixture into the centre of each flattened piece of
pastry. Using your fingertips, pull the edges together
around the filling to seal, then roll into a ball and
flatten into a 6 cm (2½ in) diameter disc. Seat aside.

To make the cakes, first preheat the oven to 180°C
(350°F/Gas 4). Pull off about one heaped teaspoon of
the bean mixture and form it into a ball by rolling it in
the palms of your hands. Place the ball into the centre
of a pastry disc and tuck the pastry edges around the
bean mixture. Seal and flatten into a round cake. Paint
a red dot of food colouring in the middle of the cake.
Repeat until you have used up all the pastry discs and
bean mixture filling.

Place the cakes on a baking sheet and bake for about
20 minutes until the pastry is cooked but not brown.
The cakes will appear soft, but will harden a little as
they cool.

Salara (Coconut Roll)

This doughy, sweet coconut bread is rarely made at home as it is sold fresh and cheaply by bicycle vendors with their glass display cases on all the main streets. It is delicious at any time of the day and much easier to make than it looks.

MAKES *12* SLICES

For the dough

1 tablespoon active dried yeast

75 ml (3 fl oz/scant ¹/₃ cup)
    warm water

85 g (3 oz/¹/₃ cup) caster (superfine)
    sugar, plus 1 teaspoon

170 ml (6 fl oz/³/₄ cup) milk

60 g (2 oz/¼ cup) lard or butter

2 teaspoons vanilla extract

675 g (1 lb 8 oz/5½ cups)
    white bread flour

vegetable oil

2 eggs, beaten

2 tablespoons melted
    unsalted butter

1 tablespoon maple syrup

For the filling

450 g (1 lb/5 cups)
    desiccated coconut

225 g (8 oz/scant 1 cup) caster
    (superfine) sugar

½ teaspoon ground allspice

½ teaspoon ground cinnamon

1 teaspoon mixed essence or
    vanilla extract

a few drops of red food colouring

To make the dough, dissolve the yeast in the warm water in a small bowl. Mix in the 1 teaspoon of sugar, cover and set aside for 10 minutes.

Warm the milk until nearly boiling, add the lard or butter, and sugar. When the fat has melted and sugar dissolved, remove from the heat and let it cool until warm, then stir in the yeast and vanilla extract.

Slowly work in the flour with your index finger until a soft dough forms. Turn it out on to a lightly floured surface and knead until it is smooth and elastic. Place the dough ball in a large mixing bowl greased with a small amount of vegetable oil and turn it around to oil all sides of the dough. Cover with clingfilm and leave in a warm place for at least 1½ hours until the dough has doubled in size. Punch the dough down, cut in half and cover and leave for 10 minutes.

Preheat the oven to 190°C (375°F/Gas 5) and combine all the ingredients for the filling, except for the red food colouring, in a mixing bowl. Add enough drops of the food colouring to turn the mixture bright red.

Roll each half of the dough into a rectangle about 1 cm (½ in) thick and measuring about 25 x 33 cm (10 x 13 in). Brush with the melted butter. Smooth half of the filling mixture over each of the rectangles but not right up to the ends. Roll the dough up lengthwise and seal the edges and leave to prove for 45 minutes. Brush the rolls with maple syrup and bake for 25–30 minutes until golden. Cool on a wire rack and serve.

Mittai

A sweet, crunchy and moreish snack, this Indo-Guyanese recipe is served at teatime and is often given away in party goody bags. I used to love sucking the crystallised sugar off the crunchy swizzles.

MAKES *12* SLICES

200 g (7 oz/1²/₃ cups) plain
   (all-purpose) flour
1 teaspoon baking powder (soda)
½ teaspoon salt
½ teaspoon ground mixed spice
vegetable oil for frying
200 g (7 oz/scant 1 cup) caster
   (superfine) sugar
½ teaspoon vanilla extract
pinch of ground nutmeg

In a large bowl, combine the flour with the baking powder, salt and mixed spice. Add enough cold water to form a dough when mixed with your index finger. Roll the dough into a sausage, cut it into small pieces and then roll each piece into strings about 5 mm (¼ in) in diameter. Cut each string into 10 cm (4 in) long strips.

Heat the oil in a deep frying pan or a deep-fat fryer until it's smoking. Drop the strips of dough into the hot oil and fry for about 1 minute or until golden. Remove them from the oil with a slotted spoon and drain on kitchen paper.

Heat the sugar with 200 ml (7 fl oz/³/₄ cup) of water in a saucepan and gently bring to the boil. When the syrup thickens, take the pan off the heat and quickly stir in the vanilla extract. Pour the syrup over the fried dough. As the syrup cools it will crystallise and form a delicious sugary, crusty coating. Dust with the nutmeg and serve.

Aunty Thelma's Chocolate Fudge

Wherever I went when I was young, people would give me great food. Aunty Thelma is one such person. She is a lovely warm-hearted smiley cousin of my father who was sadly widowed at a young age and she then moved to London from Barbados with her three children.

Whenever we went to visit her, she served up her famous sponge cake (see page 199) and would send me home with her chocolate fudge in an empty coffee jar. Her fudge has a chalky texture reminiscent of Scottish tablet, but more flavourful and not nearly as sweet. It gives me great pleasure to share this recipe with you.

MAKES *6*

4 tablespoons cocoa powder

240 ml (8½ fl oz/1 cup) milk

750 g (1 lb 10 oz/3¹/₃ cups) caster (superfine) sugar

410 g (14 oz) can evaporated milk

410 g (14 oz) can condensed milk

1 tablespoon unsalted butter

1 teaspoon vanilla extract

Whisk the cocoa powder with half of the milk and set aside. Lightly butter a 350 x 250 mm (14 x 10 in) baking tray.

Put the sugar with the remaining milk and the evaporated milk into a saucepan. Mix them together until the sugar has dissolved and then add the condensed milk and the cocoa powder/milk mix.

Heat the saucepan on a medium heat, stirring continually, and bring the liquid to the boil. Lower the heat and simmer, stirring occasionally so the liquid doesn't burn, for about 45 minutes until it has thickened.

Take the pan off the heat and add the butter and vanilla extract. Continue to stir for a couple of minutes, then return the pan to the heat for another minute before pouring the now thickened mixture into the prepared dish and leave it to set. Cut the chocolate fudge into cubes and serve.

Guava Brown Betty

This buttery, sweet dish is wonderful served with custard, and makes the perfect pudding for a cold winter's night.

Preheat the oven to 180°C (350°F/Gas 4) and grease a baking dish.

Gently melt the butter in a saucepan over a medium heat, then stir in the breadcrumbs and set aside.

Drain the guavas and combine with the sugar, mixed spice and vanilla extract. Lay half of the guava mixture on the bottom of the prepared baking dish, cover with half the breadcrumb mixture and repeat.

Bake for about 25 minutes until the breadcrumbs are golden. Pour over the lime juice and serve with custard, cream or ice cream.

85 g (3 oz) unsalted butter

200 g (7 oz/2½ cups) fresh breadcrumbs

450 g (14 oz) can stewed guavas in syrup

75 g (2½ oz/¹/₃ cup) demerara sugar

1 teaspoon mixed spice

1 teaspoon vanilla extract

juice of 1 lime

Cassavapon

Serve with vanilla ice cream or rum sauce or, better still, a glass of June's Rum Punch (see page 232). If you don't want to use the lard then substitute it with butter.

SERVES 8

1 teaspoon vegetable oil

450 g (1 lb/5 cups) desiccated coconut

900 g (2 lb) grated cassava

175 g (6 oz) caster (superfine) sugar

60 g (2 oz/¼ cup) salted butter, melted (plus a little extra for sprinkling over the top)

60 g (2 oz/¼ cup) lard, melted

225 g (8 oz/generous 1¾ cups) raisins

1 teaspoon vanilla extract

1 teaspoon grated fresh ginger

½ teaspoon ground nutmeg

½ teaspoon ground cinnamon

½ teaspoon ground cloves

1 teaspoon salt

1 teaspoon freshly ground black pepper

1 tablespoon demerara sugar

Preheat the oven to 180°C (350°F/Gas 4).

Grease a shallow baking tray with the vegetable oil.

Combine the grated coconut, cassava and sugar together, with the melted butter and lard, if using.

Add the water mix and bind. Add the fruit, vanilla extract, ginger, spices, salt and pepper and mix well.

Pour the mixture into the prepared baking tray and sprinkle with flecks of butter over the top along with the demerara sugar.

Bake for 1–1½ hours until the top is golden brown and crispy.

Allow to rest and cool. Cut into squares or rectangles and serve with vanilla ice cream or rum sauce.

Pineapple and Coconut Tart

MAKES *6-8* SLICES

For shortcrust pastry base

225 g (8 oz/1²/³ cups) flour

60 g (2 oz/¼ cup) unsalted
butter, cubed

60 g (2 oz/¼ cup) lard, cubed
pinch of salt

pinch of mixed spice

2–3 tablespoons ice-cold water

For the pie filling

40 g (1½ oz/¹/³ cup) flour

185 g (6½ oz/1 cup lightly packed)
soft brown sugar

3 eggs, lightly beaten

250 ml (8½ fl oz/1 cup)
maple syrup

100 g (3½ oz/generous 1 cup)
desiccated coconut

225 g (8 oz) can pineapple,
chopped

1 teaspoon Caribbean
mixed essence

½ teaspoon mixed spice

60 g (2 oz/¼ cup) unsalted
butter, melted

To make the pastry, put the flour, butter and lard into a mixing bowl and rub together until they resemble breadcrumbs. Sprinkle in the salt and mixed spice, then add the ice-cold water. Use a knife to mix the ingredients into a dough and when it coms away from the sides of the bowl, form it into a ball, wrap it in clingfilm and refrigerate for 30 minutes.

Pre heat the oven to 180°C (350°F/Gas 5) prepare a 25 cm (10 in) diameter loose-bottomed flan tin.

Unwrap the pastry and roll it out on a floured surface into a round about 5 mm (¼ in) thick. Line the prepared flan tin with the pastry, prick the base all over with a fork and trim the edges. Cover with baking parchment and fill with baking beans and bake blind for 15 minutes.

Meanwhile, to make the filling, combine the flour and sugar in a mixing bowl. Mix in the eggs, maple syrup, coconut, pineapple, mixed essence and mixed spice.

When the pastry case is ready, remove it from the oven and lift off the baking parchment with its baking beans. Pour the filling into the pastry case and drizzle the melted butter over the top. Bake on the middle shelf for about 50 minutes until it is golden and a knife inserted into the centre comes out clean.

Serve with a dollop of fresh cream.

Caribbean Pavlova with Rum Sauce

Preheat the oven to 130°C (250°F/Gas) and line a baking tray with greaseproof paper.

For the meringue, put the egg whites into a mixing bowl and whisl until soft peaks form. Add half the sugar and continue to whisk until the peaks are stiff and silkily glossy. Then gradually whisk in the remaining sugar followed by sifted cornflour, vinegar and Caribbean essence.

Spread the meringue mixture over the greaseproof paper and, using the back of a metal spoon, make a slight hollow in the centre for the filling to go in later. Bake the meringue for 1 hour or until it is crisp on the outside and chewy and soft in the middle. Turn off the oven and allow the meringue to cool in the oven until you are ready to fill it.

To make the filling, gently whisk the double cream until soft peaks appear. Add the sugar, sherry and Caribbean essence and continue to whisk until the cream is to your desired consistency. Spread the cream over the meringue hollow, then place the cut fruit over the cream and squeeze the passion fruit over the top.

For the sauce, put the sugar and butter in a saucepan over a medium heat and stir until the butter is melted and the sauce becomes smooth. Take the pan off the heat and whisk in the double cream, liqueur and mixed spice. Return the pan to the heat and simmer for 5 minutes or until the sauce is reduced and glossy. Pour the sauce into a jug, cover with clingfilm and leave to cool. Pour the sauce over the meringue before serving.

For the meringue base

4 egg whites

225 g (8 oz/1 cup) caster
   (superfine) sugar

2 teaspoons cornflour (cornstarch)

2 teaspoons white wine vinegar

1 teaspoon mixed Caribbean
   mixed essence

For the filling

300 ml (10 fl oz/1¼ cups) double
   (thick) cream

2 tablespoons caster
   (superfine) sugar

2 tablespoons cream sherry
   or dark rum

1 teaspoon Caribbean
   mixed essence

1 ripe mango, diced

1 kiwi fruit, sliced into half moons

225 g (8 oz) can pineapple chunks

2 passion fruit, halved

For the sauce

225 g (8 oz/1 cup) demerara sugar

115 g (31/2 oz/scant ½ cup)
   unsalted butter

170 ml (6 fl oz/³/₄ cup) double
   (thick) cream

3 tablespoons coconut liqueur

1 teaspoon mixed spice

Pumpkin Fritters

These are fabulous served with rum and raisin ice cream and a drizzle of maple syrup.

MAKES *12*

450 g (1 lb/3 cups) finely grated
    pumpkin (squash)

2 eggs, beaten

120 ml (4 fl oz/½ cup) milk

60 g (2 oz/¼ cup) salted
    butter, melted

60 g (2 oz/¼ cup) demerara sugar

1 teaspoon vanilla extract

175 g (6 oz/1½ cups)
    self-raising flour

½ teaspoon ground cinnamon

½ teaspoon ground allspice

oil for frying

Put the pumpkin in a bowl together with the eggs, milk, butter, sugar and vanilla extract. Then add the flour, cinnamon and allspice and beat everything into a thick batter.

Heat 1 tablespoon of oil in a frying pan over a medium-low heat. Drop the batter into the pan, a tablespoon at a time, in batches of 4, and cook for 2–3 minutes on each side until golden. Drain on kitchen paper and keep warm. Repeat with the rest of the batter, adding more oil if necessary.

Aunty Bonnie's Lemon Drizzle

Aunty Bonnie and Uncle Budsey were like Father and Mother Christmas to me and visits to see them and my cousins number among some of my happiest childhood memories. I was the youngest of eight cousins and was teased, spoiled and overfed. We would dance to the reggae greatest hits and eat an array of goodies from Aunty Bonnie's kitchen. Aunty Bonnie seemed to spend most of her time in her kitchen. My cousins would appear with trays of various goodies and no visit was complete until I felt that I was as full as an egg! I miss them both for their kindness, generosity and delicious goody bags. This is but one of Aunty Bonnie's specialities.

SERVES 4

Preheat the oven to 180°C (350°F/Gas 4) and butter and line a 20 cm (8 in) diameter cake tin.

Cream the margarine and sugar in a bowl with a handheld electric mixer until they are pale. Mix in the eggs, one at a time, beating well between each addition, and then fold in the lemon zest, flour and baking powder and add the milk. Beat for 3 minutes until everything is well combined.

Pour the batter into the prepared cake tin and bake for 50–60 minutes until the cake has shrunk form the sides and the cake is firm in the middle when gently pressed with a finger. Leave the cake in the tin.

For the icing, mix the sugars with the lemon juice in a bowl until blended. Spread the mixture over the top of the cake as soon as it has finished baking and still hot. Leave the cake in the tin until cooled, then turn out and serve with whipped cream.

115 g (3½ oz) soft margarine
175 g (6 oz/³/₄ cup) caster (superfine) sugar
2 eggs
grated zest of 1 lemon
175 g (6 oz/1½ cups) self-raising flour
1 teaspoon baking powder (soda)
4 tablespoons milk

For the icing
115 g (3½ oz/½ cup) caster (superfine) sugar
2 tablespoons icing sugar, sifted
juice of 1 lemon

Coconut Rock Buns

MAKES *12–14* BUNS

225 g (8 oz/1¾ cups) plain
    (all-purpose) flour
1 teaspoon baking powder (soda)
80 g (3 oz/scant ½ cup) unsalted
    butter, cubed
115 g (3½ oz/½ cup firmly packed)
    brown sugar
½ teaspoon mixed spice
pinch of salt
100 g (3½ oz/generous 1 cup)
    desiccated coconut
80 g (3 oz/scant ½ cup) dried
    mixed fruit
50 g (2 oz/¼ cup) chopped
maraschino cherries, plus
    7 halved cherries to decorate
1 egg, beaten
1 teaspoon Caribbean
    mixed essence
4 tablespoons milk

Preheat the oven to 180°C (350°F/Gas 4) and butter and flour a baking tray.

Sift the flour and baking powder into a mixing bowl, add the butter and rub together until they resemble breadcrumbs. Add the sugar and mixed spice, salt, dessicated coconut, dried mixed fruit and maraschino cherries and mix well. Then add the beaten egg and mixed essence and 2 tablespoons of the milk to bind the ingredients into a stiff dough, adding the remaining milk if the mixture is too stiff.

Drop 12–14 generous teaspoons of the mixture on to the prepared baking tray, top each bun with a halved maraschino cherry and bake for 20 minutes until golden.

Margery's Sunflower Biscuits

MAKES *12* BISCUITS

450 g (1 lb/3½ cups) plain
    (all-purpose) flour

2 pinches of salt

225 g (8 oz/scant 1 cup) lard
    or butter

4–6 tablespoons ice-cold water

175 g (6 oz/generous ⅔ cup)
    smooth peanut butter

175 g (6 oz/generous ¾ cup)
    granulated sugar

1 teaspoon Caribbean
    mixed essence

red food colouring for decorating

2 eggs, beaten with
    2 tablespoons milk

Preheat the oven to 180°C (350°F/Gas 4) and butter a baking sheet.

Sift the flour into a mixing bowl, add the salt and the lard or butter and rub together until they resemble breadcrumbs. Then add the ice-cold water, a little at a time, and combine until the pastry forms a ball. With floured hands, roll the dough into a sausage, cut into 12 equal parts and roll into balls. Set aside.

To make the filling, mix the peanut butter with the sugar and mixed essence. Flatten the balls into discs in the palm of your hands and fill each one with 1 teaspoon of the filling. Seal up the edges and pat flat.

Paint a red dot on the middle of each disc and let the food colouring dry. Then put twelve incisions in the pastries along the edge of the red dot and twist to the right.

Brush each biscuit with egg wash and place on the prepared baking sheet. Bake for 15–20 minutes until golden brown. Remove from the oven and let the biscuits cool before serving.

Pineapple Upsidedown Cake

My father loved winding my mother up by comparing her dessert skills to his mother, aunts and sisters. Fortunately, Mum knew that her upside down cake always looked and tasted great. Whenever she served it, we knew that Dad would stay happy and no one would get into trouble. In my opinion, there are several recipes that taste better when made with margarine and this is one of them. However, you can easily substitute it with lightly salted butter.

MAKES *12*

Preheat the oven to 180°C (350°F/Gas 4) and grease a 23 cm (9 in) round cake tin.

For the topping, melt the margarine or butter in a small saucepan over a medium heat. Add all the ingedients except for the pineapples and cherries and stir. Gently simmer until the sauce begins to thicken. Remove from the heat and leave it to cool slightly.

Pour the sauce into the tin. Brush some of the topping a quarter way up the sides of the tin. Lay the pineapple rings on the base of the tin and put a cherry in the centre of each ring.

For the cake, cream the margarine or butter and sugar in a mixing bowl until light. Beat in the vanilla extract and half of the beaten eggs, then fold in half of the flour and semolina alternately together with the remaining eggs, the milk and the pineapple syrup. Spread the cake mixture over the fruit and bake for 45 minutes or until the cake has risen and is golden.

Meanwhile, make the cream by mixing all the ingredients together in a bowl. When the cake is ready, remove it from the oven and allow it to cool slightly before turning out onto a plate. Serve cut into slices with a spoonful of the cream.

For the topping

120 g (4 oz/½ cup) margarine or butter

120 g (4 oz/½ cup) demerara (raw) sugar

4 tablespoons dark rum

2 teaspoons ground allspice

7 small pineapple rings, drained (reserve the syrup)

7 glacé cherries

For the cake

150 g (5 oz/²/₃ cup) margarine or butter

150 g (5 oz/²/₃ cup) caster (superfine) sugar

1½ teaspoons vanilla extract

4 large eggs, lightly beaten

225 g (8 oz/1³/₄ cups) self-raising flour

50 g (2 oz/generous ¹/₃ cup) fine semolina

3 tablespoons milk

3 tablespoons pineapple syrup from can

For the rum and vanilla spike cream

300 ml (10 fl oz/1¼ cups) double cream

½ vanilla pod, cut in half lengthways and seeds scraped out

1 tablespoon dark rum

1 tablespoon caster (superfine) sugar

Carambola Bread and Butter Pudding with a Guava Glaze

What a delicious combination of classic British and Caribbean flavours this pudding is. The mere smell of it baking evokes the happiest of family and childhood memories. Carambola also known as starfruit and makes a great filling for this hearty pudding.

SERVES 4-6

Preheat the oven to 180°C (370°F/Gas 4).

Put the chopped starfruit in a small saucepan and add 1 tablespoon of the demerara sugar, 2 tablespoons of the dark rum and the mixed essence. Bring to the boil, then reduce the heat and simmer for 15 minutes. Set aside and cool.

Pour the milk and cream into a deep baking dish. Add the eggs and egg yolks and whisk until well combined. Then add the caster sugar, mixed fruit, vanilla extract, allspice and cinnamon and whisk together. Pour the cooled stewed fruit and its cooking liquor into the baking dish and mix well with a fork.

Butter the bread on both sides and cut off the crusts. Then cut the bread into triangles and arrange over the dish with edges overlapping. Push it down so that the bread is well soaked. Sprinkle the top with the remaining demerara sugar and bake in the oven for 30 minutes until lightly golden.

For the topping, gently melt the guava jelly in a pan and mix in the remaining rum. With a pastry brush, spread the jelly evenly over the top of the pudding to glaze. Return the pudding to the oven and bake for a further 20 minutes, until golden brown and the custard is set.

2 starfruit (carambola), 1 chopped and the other sliced

2 tablespoons demerara sugar

3 tablespoons dark rum

1 teaspoon Caribbean mixed essence

450 ml (15 fl oz/scant 2 cups) milk

300 ml (10 fl oz/1¼ cups) double (thick) cream

2 eggs plus 2 egg yolks

60 g (2 oz/¼ cup) caster (superfine) sugar

175 g (6 oz/scant 1 cup) dried mixed fruit

2 teaspoons vanilla extract

1 teaspoon ground allspice

½ teaspoon ground cinnamon

60 g (2 oz/¼ cup) unsalted butter

5–6 slices of stale white bread

2 tablespoons guava jelly

7 Thirsty Work

Brandy Alexander

Brandy Alexander's were introduced to me by my Uncle Bertie, Cecile's father and one of my grandfather, Cyril's, best friends. Bertie was a bon vivant, a gentleman and the life and soul of any party. He had a booming voice and an infectious laugh. Indeed, his dinner parties were legendary throughout the Caribbean.

Uncle Bertie loved spicy food, but as he got older he found that he had less tolerance for hot curries and so, for medicinal purposes, he would drink a Brandy Alexander before, during and after a curry. Bertie Dumett died on 17 August 1984, aged 84.

On a recent trip to Tobago I cooked with a wonderful chef named Nick Hardwicke who owns the highly regarded Seahorse Inn. He introduced me to his parents, who had spent time in Guyana in the sixties and seventies and subsequently moved around the Caribbean and settled in Tobago. They said that of all the places in the Caribbean where they had lived, they found the people in Georgetown, were without the question, the friendliest and the most hospitable.

Because Georgetown had few restaurants, people entertained you in their homes and, as they always expected guests of varying nationalities, their tables were laden with food from the six nations that make up the Caribbean. On mentioning Uncle Bertie's name, Mrs Hardwicke's eyes filled with tears and she told me how kind Bertie had been to her and her husband over many years and how much they and missed their dear friend and then she remembered how wonderful his dinner parties were.

Simultaneously we asked, 'Brandy Alexander anyone?!' and collapsed into fits of laughter. At that moment, for a split second, I swear that I could hear Bertie laughing too, but it was probably just the ocean.

MAKES *2* COCKTAILS

Put the brandy, cream and crème de cacao in a cocktail shaker together with crushed ice.

Shake well until combined and then strain into two martini glasses and decorate with the grated nutmeg.

120 ml (4 fl oz/½ cup) brandy
120 ml (4 fl oz/½ cup) cream
120 ml (4 fl oz/½ cup) crème de cacao
250 g (9 oz) crushed ice
freshly grated nutmeg

Uncle Bertie loved spicy food, but as he got older he found that he had less tolerance for hot curries and so, for medicinal purposes, he would drink a Brandy Alexander before, during and after a curry!

June's Rum Punch

Two words that sum up June are life and soul and spending time with her is a joy. She and mum must have been a pair of horrors at St Rose's! June is a wonderful cook mother and friend. Her rum punch is guaranteed to liven up the dullest of do's!

MAKES *10* COCKTAILS

225 g (8 oz/1 cup) caster
    (superfine) sugar
225 ml (8 fl oz/1 cup) lime
    or lemon juice
juice of 2 oranges
800 ml (27 fl oz/3¼ oz) dark rum
3 tablespoons Grenadine
4 drops of Angostura bitters
½ teaspoon grated nutmeg
plenty of ice cubes
finely sliced orange

Make a sugar syrup by putting the sugar in a saucepan with 450 ml (15 fl oz/scant 2 cups) of water. Gently bring to the boil and then boil rapidly for about 2 minutes, stirring, until the sugar is dissolved. Set aside to cool.

In large bowl or jug, combine the fruit juices with the cooled sugar syrup, rum and Grenadine and stir well. Add the bitters and nutmeg.

Serve in a tall glass over plenty of ice and garnish with finely sliced orange.

Vodka Lime Rickey

My father introduced me to this cocktail at The American Bar in The Savoy. He had taken us as a family to experience 'the better things in life' with the hope that we would become more ambitious. Sadly, all it did was give me a lifelong taste for vodka!

MAKES *10* COCKTAILS

225 g (8 oz/1 cup) caster
    (superfine) sugar
1 teaspoon finely grated
    fresh ginger
juice of 6 limes
375 ml (12 fl oz/1½ cups) vodka
375 ml (12 fl oz/1½ cups) soda water
plenty of ice cubes
Angostura bitters, pineapple
    slices, lime slices, maraschino
    cherries and mint leaves
    to garnish

Make a sugar syrup by putting the sugar and ginger in a saucepan with 225 g (8 oz/1 cup) of water. Gently bring to the boil and then boil rapidly for about 2 minutes, stirring, until the sugar is dissolved. Set aside to cool.

Pour the lime juice, vodka and syrup into a tall jug and mix well. Add the soda water and plenty of ice just before serving.

Garnish with a few drops of Angostura bitters, pineapple slices, slices, or lime slices, maraschino cherries and mint leaves.

Chevy

This is as delicious as it is lethal! A grown-up punch with plenty of kick.

MAKES *10* COCKTAILS

2 tablespoons Southern Comfort

2 tablespoons Crown Royal whisky

2 tablespoons amaretto liqueur

60 ml (2 fl oz/¼ cup)
    pineapple juice

60 ml (2 fl oz/¼ cup) orange juice

plenty of ice cubes

dash of Grenadine

orange slices and maraschino
cherries to garnish

Mix the spirits together and top with the pineapple and orange juices.

Serve over ice, add a dash of Grenadine and garnish with the orange slices and maraschino cherries.

Pina Colada

This filling cocktail is an ideal substitute for dessert and makes me think of fun lazy days, lounging by a pool without a care in the world.

MAKES 2 COCKTAILS

120 ml (4 fl oz/½ cup)
    pineapple juice
120 ml (4 fl oz/½ cup) white rum
60 ml (2 fl oz/¼ cup) coconut cream
500 g (1 lb 2 oz) crushed ice
pineapple slices and
    maraschino cherries

Mix the spirits together and top with the pineapple and orange juices.

Serve over ice, add a dash of Grenadine and garnish with the orange slices and maraschino cherries.

I was the youngest of three children and no one really had the time to play with me, so I spent all of my spare time in the kitchen experimenting with food, with its textures, colours and smells, and I loved it.

Index

Female visitors
they sat around
love and home.
tales and their
the main meal.
make pastry tr
approval and g
brought them

ned Mum and me in the kitchen where

table and talked non-stop about life.

stened to all of this. absorbing their

sip. Then. when Mum had finished cooking

uld come into my own and bake a cake or

I found that my creations won me

e something to hide behind as I

the front room for the men to eat.

Acknowledgements

I would like to thank the following people for their support, belief and enthusiasm during the writing of this book:

Stephen King, Kate Pollard, Kajal Mistry, Caroline Brown and Jennifer Seymour at Hardie Grant for their commitment, expertise and for making my dreams come true.

Jacqui Melville, Nicole Herft and Jessica Mills for making my recipes come alive and look so appetising and professional.

My wonderful team at Debbie Walter's Management. David Evans, Linda Scheur, Alison Hayes and all of our fabulous artists for their patience and support.

Pip Vice for teaching me so much and inspiring my confidence.

Sacha Brooks , Rena Brannan, Tania Bryer, Lisa Butcher Edmund Butt, Harriet Close, Cy Chadwick, Martina Cole, John Davis, Jody Dunleavy, William Forde, Mary Fitzpatrick, Janice Gabriel, Julie Gallagher, Lulu Grimes, Jerry Hall, Nigel Hall, Ruby Hammer, Diana Howie, Clare Hollywood, Carla-Maria Lawson, Peter Lang, Hilary Murray, Dale Pring, Lee Pring, James Thompson, Nick Thorogood, John Reid, Barry Ryan, Sue Walton and Sophie Ward.

Leith's School of Food and Wine, Optomen Television and Shine Tv.

Dale Pring Mac Sweeney, who painted the opposite picture.

With special thanks and all my love to Christopher Jerez and Olivia.

Jonathan Phang has worked in the fashion industry for over two decades and continues to manage the careers of some of the biggest names in the business. He appears on television as a fashion expert, noticeably as a judge on Britain and Ireland's Next Top Model. As well as his fashion credentials, Jonathan has a long standing passion for food and cooking. He currently hosts Jonathan Phang's Caribbean Cookbook, for Food Network and the Travel Channel, based on his Caribbean recipes. He lives in London.

...ines. It is an asset in life to be a
...ial success, & if you have prov...
...friendship you should take
...care not to ~~blos~~ nourish &
...we it. It wouldn't do to
...ke friends today & lose the...
...row — in that case you are
...ailure socially. You should
...Books on Psychology & under...
...others better — copy Budsey
...at score & with a natural
...harm you should have a happy
...istence.

...shall be Home soon, but up t...
...ow I cannot say it will be for
...mas. With lots of Love from
Mom & Dad.

...shall make all enquiries concerni...
...unaccompanied baggage & when the...
...will reach B.G., & will send key fo...
same later.

The Pepperpot Club by Jonathan Phang

First published in 2013 by Hardie Grant Books

Hardie Grant Books London
Dudley House, North Suite
34–35 Southampton Street
London WC2E 7HF
www.hardiegrant.co.uk

Hardie Grant Books (Australia)
Ground Floor, Building 1
658 Church Street
Melbourne, VIC 3121
www.hardiegrant.com.au

British Library Cataloguing-in-Publication Data. A catalogue record
for this book is available from the British Library.

ISBN 978-1-74270-556-9

Commissioning Editor: Kate Pollard
Desk Editor: Kajal Mistry
Food photography and retouching by Jacqui Melville
Food styling by Nicole Herft
Internal design by Two Associates
Cover illustration and Design by Joseph Vass (www.josephvass.com)
Colour reproduction by p2d

Printed and bound China by 1010 Printing International Limited

10 9 8 7 6 5 4 3 2 1